Revolution, A Love Story

There is a better way!

By Cindy Sheehan with foreword by Eva Golinger

Dear Bobbie,
Thanks for all the wonderful hospitality, the ride from Colton, the water workout, comfy bed, & all the other comforts of a nice home.
Keep strong!
Love & Peace
Cindy Sheehan

Revolution, a Love Story:
There is a better way!

By Cindy Sheehan

Foreword by Eva Golinger

Acknowledgments

A)   Albert Einstein on Socialism

B)   Interviews:

    i.   Hugo Chávez

    ii.   Cynthia McKinney

    iii.   Gore Vidal

    iv.   Eva Golinger

    v.   Ed Asner

    vi.   Angela Davis

    vii.   Robert Fisk

    viii.   Temir Porras

C)   LIST OF FINANCIAL SPONSORS ($50 OR MORE)

FOREWORD

EVA GOLINGER

A Voice of Truth in the Belly of the Beast

I first met Cindy Sheehan when she came to Caracas in January 2006 for the World Social Forum. An event of that size and stature had never taken place in Venezuela before as Caracas became the host to tens of thousands of international guests immersed in a frenzy of politics, activism, debate, dissent, and revolution. Of all the distinguished, admired, and well known attendees, Cindy was at the top of the list.

President Hugo Chávez had spoken highly and often about Cindy Sheehan, praising her brave fight against the Bush administration and her fervent opposition to the war in Iraq, which had caused the death of her son, Casey. Before Cindy Sheehan ever came to Venezuela, the people of this South American nation had heard her name many times. We knew of her political transformation after Casey died and her unwavering commitment to peace and justice. We'd heard of her valiantly defying President George W. Bush by setting up "Camp Casey" outside his Texas ranch, demanding the United States president answer for his crimes, and advocating for an end to war. President Chávez invoked Cindy Sheehan as a symbol of good-hearted, honest people in the United States willing to risk their lives to fight injustice, despite the arrogance and hostility emanating from the US government.

So when Cindy first came to Caracas, she was in high demand by Venezuelan media. The host of one of the country's most watched morning programs, Ernesto Villegas, contacted me about interviewing Cindy during her stay in Venezuela. While I had never met the Peace Mom personally, I figured the world of revolutionaries from the United States is—unfortunately—small enough, so I must know someone close to her. I was right and Cindy kindly agreed to do the live interview.

Since I had helped arrange the interview, I accompanied Cindy to the special television studio, which had been set up outside the main venue of the World Social Forum. The program host was ecstatic with Cindy's presence, particularly after conducting many shows on Washington's illegal war against Iraq, and referring often to the US peace movement and Cindy's own battle against Bush. One minor logistical detail had gone overlooked: Cindy did not speak Spanish and the show's host did not speak English.

While I am not a translator by profession, I have found myself serving in such a capacity numerous times over the past decade, especially when it comes to Venezuela. I have spontaneously been whisked into the role of translator to interpret discussions and interviews for President Hugo Chávez during his many trips to New York or when visitors have come to Venezuela from the United States. And, I have also now had the unexpected honor of translating for Cindy Sheehan during her various visits to Venezuela.

So, I was Cindy Sheehan's translator during her first live television interview in Venezuela. As I translated her responses to questions about the war against Iraq, Bush administration policies and violations of the US Constitution, and issues relating to social justice, I felt as though the answers were coming from me. (Don't worry Cindy, I really did translate you). The words flowed from her with a sincerity, honesty, and frankness in a way that I hadn't heard from a US person in a long time.

That same sincere, honest, and direct tone shines throughout her dialogue with readers in this book, *Revolution: A Love Story.* Cindy's honesty is what sets her apart from many others in the United States who, while disagreeing with Bush's— and now Obama's—policies, dare not to raise their voices or speak their minds for fear of reprisal. And Cindy's fearlessness is what terrified President George W. Bush, and Washington defenders, and turned her into a role model for justice and peace seekers around the world.

Four years after my first job as translator for Cindy Sheehan, I was surprised into the role again, but this time it wasn't for live television, it was with President Chávez.

When Cindy decided she wanted to make a documentary film and write a book on Venezuela's Revolution and she contacted me for advice, I was more than eager to help. Cindy Sheehan has been a solid, powerful ally for Venezuela's Bolivarian Revolution and President Chávez for many years, despite the attacks, threats, and criticisms she has had to bear.

Cindy's voice, as it flows throughout the following pages, serenades readers with her stories and experiences inside Venezuela as a witness to the vibrant process of transformation taking place. The greatest value in Cindy's words is precisely that they come from her own personal experiences. Instead of believing what media said about Venezuela and President Chávez, Cindy came to find out for herself. She met with different people and heard their stories and testimonies. She went into their communities and witnessed their lives, seeing with her own eyes whether things were better or worse. Cindy has seen, touched, and breathed the Bolivarian Revolution. She speaks truth from experience.

I didn't hesitate to help when Cindy requested an interview with President Chávez for this important project. Arrangements were made and Cindy soon set foot once again in the land of Simón Bolívar. I accompanied Cindy during her brief stay in Caracas (where I reside) in late February 2010, and we visited some of the amazing achievements of the Revolution. Despite her fear of heights, she rode in the newly inaugurated MetroCable in the San Agustin neighborhood of Caracas.

The cable car was the first of a series being built by the Chávez administration throughout the Caracas metropolitan area, which is flanked by steep hills and mountain ranges covered in hard-to-reach makeshift homes, primarily occupied by the poor and working class. The MetroCable was a lifesaver to many in San Agustin, which is one of Caracas' oldest and primarily Afro-Venezuelan neighborhoods. Built and run by workers from the community and paid for by the state, it services thousands who previously had to walk miles up steep and dangerous roads and steps built in the hillsides, or take shoddy jeeps and vans posing as "public transport" up the mountain, until they could go no further and the only way to proceed was on foot. The elderly and disabled rarely left their homes before the MetroCable was installed.

Cindy bore witness to this transformative project created by the Bolivarian Revolution, seeing and hearing how it changed community members' lives dramatically. Not only were their daily lives made easier by the new and innovative transport system, but it also brought dignity and pride to their community. They built it, they run it, and they are no longer overlooked or ignored by those in power or those with more money. The MetroCable of San Agustin is emblematic of the way President Hugo Chávez's leadership and the Bolivarian Revolution have changed Venezuela forever.

The millions of invisible people in Venezuela are now visible. The millions silenced before now have a voice, and they speak loud and clear. Participatory democracy is a wonderful thing.

When it came time for Cindy to interview President Chávez, he invited her to accompany him on a trip to Montevideo, Uruguay, for the historical inauguration of newly-elected President José "Pepe" Mujica, a former guerrilla fighter and political prisoner who had been tortured, imprisoned, and shot over a dozen times in the 1970s.

Chávez is known for preferring to do interviews with foreign press while flying or during an international trip. He's so overly-dedicated to his work for the Venezuelan people and the future of Venezuela that he feels there is no time to spare for any other activities while in-country. So he squeezes in the interviews on long plane trips, or during brief moments between events while in another country, where often he has less control over his own agenda.

I happened to attend an event where President Chávez was speaking on the day of Cindy's arrival to Caracas, and at the end of his intervention, I caught up with him and reminded him Cindy would be in town for a few days before the Uruguay trip. I told him she was doing a documentary on the Revolution and so I'd be taking her around to several communities to meet with different grassroots organizations and dialogue with community activists. "Tell her: *Welcome to Venezuela!* for me." he responded. "Oh, and then you should come with us, too, to Uruguay", he quickly added as an aside.

It wasn't until we were on the presidential aircraft two days later heading to Montevideo that I realized I would once again be translator for Cindy and President Chávez. Even more surprisingly, I ended up being Bolivian President Evo Morales' translator too after he appeared unexpectedly in the middle of Cindy's interview with Chávez!

And even though translating is not my profession, I have been more than honored to be Cindy Sheehan's interpreter, however many times are necessary.

Revolution: A Love Story provides readers with an easy-to-read background of Washington's interventionist policies in Latin

America and the rise of Revolution south of the border. Cindy's words flow as though she's talking right to you, sharing this tale over strong black Venezuelan coffee, or a delicious glass of Argentine Malbec. She provides a brief, but necessary, summary of Venezuela's contemporary history and explains how and why the Bolivarian Revolution exists, and who the charismatic and soulful man who leads it really is.

Cindy weaves in testimonies, quotes, and excerpts of interviews with a range of important and knowledgeable voices that not only provide insight into Venezuela's reality, but also help deconstruct US foreign and domestic policy.

I know why this book is called *Revolution: A Love Story.*

While you, the reader, may have only heard about Venezuela and President Chávez through international media, which tells high tales of dictatorships, human rights violations, tyrants, political prisoners, censorship, violent crime, narco-traffickers, and terrorists, I have lived in the dynamic, inclusive, open, participatory democracy in Venezuela. I have had the privilege of participating in the numerous transparent, efficient, and free electoral processes over the past decade, the majority of which Chávez and his party have won by landslide victories. I have been a face amongst the crowds of millions that frequently rally, march, and celebrate the extraordinary achievements of the Bolivarian Revolution and the policies enacted by President Hugo Chávez. Yes, Venezuelans don't just protest when they are unhappy, they also take to the streets to show support for positive advances and gains, evidencing the people's ongoing and important role in government.

While mass media portray President Hugo Chávez as a dictator, or an enraged demon, or a clown or a terrorist, I know the man with the largest heart I've ever seen. I know the man who listens to the older woman who grabs his arm and pulls him close, telling him of her woes; the man who hugs a young pregnant woman, gently cradling her belly, promising to ensure her the best care possible; the man who orders his caravan to stop on the side of the road while he rescues a stray, limping dog; the man who has given his life, his heart, and his soul to his people and his homeland and pledged to do everything in his power to help build a proud, sovereign, grandiose, and dignified nation.

And while most media ignore the millions of Venezuelans struggling to free themselves from centuries of cultural, economic, and political colonization, fighting to rescue their own identity and self-respect and to transform their country into a prosperous and flourishing nation, I know this kind, humble people that are the backbone of one of the greatest and most inspiring revolutions of our time.

During the Washington-backed coup d'etat in April 2002 that briefly and violently ousted President Chávez from power—demolishing the country's democratic institutions and plummetting the nation into a repressive dictatorship installed by the old school elite—it wasn't anger that drove millions into the streets to fight back, it was love. It was love for the true freedom that had just began to blossom with the onset of the Bolivarian Revolution in 1999. It was love for the vibrant, active, and inclusive democracy being built by, for, and of the people. It was love for the dream of an independent, sovereign, and socially prosperous Patria Grande that was being attained. And it was love for the person who had given everything of himself to forge this path that in turn made the people risk their lives to rescue him from the hands of death.

As Uncle Sam sneered, President Hugo Chávez was saved by the millions of Venezuelans who poured into the streets on April 13, 2002 to fight back against the US-funded and supported coup. His life was rescued from the point of assassination by the humble, noble majority of Venezuelans who fought against the world's most powerful empire, armed with nothing but dignity and love. And they won. We won.

That love, as cheesy as it may sound, has been the guiding force of the Bolivarian Revolution throughout the past decade. It's the same force that has created a government of People's Power, where social justice reigns and people's needs are prioritized over profits. It's not perfect—there are many problems and goals yet to be achieved. There have been many mistakes along the way, and there are many more errors to be made. Building a better world is not an easy thing.

Venezuela's Revolution does not pretend to copy or be like any other, nor does it pretend to have all the answers already drawn up. We are building block upon block, and sometimes on circles or triangles. It is a patient, human process that accepts its errors, learns from them, and continues moving forward.

As powerful as love is, the threats against Venezuela and President Chávez are numerous and scary. Washington has been waging an aggressive campaign—which could be considered a form of warfare—against the Chávez administration for over a decade. The Obama administration has intensified hostility against Venezuela, channeling even more millions of US taxpayer dollars to the anti-Chávez opposition and attempting to include Venezuela on its "state sponsors of terrorism" list in order to justify military intervention. Sanctions have been imposed against Venezuela by the White House and countless statements have been made by State Department spokespeople intending to intimidate and pressure the Venezuelan government so it succumbs to Washington's agenda.

There are critical presidential elections in Venezuela in October 2012. President Chávez is a candidate for reelection. In addition to confronting the external threats from Washington and the internal destabilization attempts executed by opposition forces, Chávez is battling the most powerful enemy he's ever had: Cancer. While the Venezuelan President has recovered impressively from a cancerous tumor extracted from his pelvic region in June 2011, his health will continue to be a battleground.

Revolution: A Love Story is a critical book to read for people around the world, but especially those in the United States. Deconstructing the dangerous myths about Venezuela is essential to preserving not only the integrity of a nation and a political process, but also the lives of millions of people. We all saw how fast a leader was demonized in mass media, stories of atrocities were spun, bombs began, thousands were killed, a nation was destroyed, and its leader assassinated in the case of Libya.

It horrifies me to remember that, just months before the war against Libya began, I had accompanied President Chávez on a trip to Tripoli, where we met with Muammar al-Gaddafi. We walked the streets of a peaceful nation and saw children playing in parks, people going shopping, families taking walks. It's sickening to realize just days later, they were killed and maimed by US bombs, in the name of freedom.

It terrifies me to think the same thing could happen in Venezuela. The same thing could happen anywhere.

Voices of truth, voices like Cindy Sheehan's, are essential to prevent these barbaric acts from reoccurring. Thank you, Cindy, for your fearlessness, for your honesty, and for your love.

Eva Golinger

Caracas, Venezuela

2012

INTRODUCTION

The history of Latin America's underdevelopment is an integral part of the history of world capitalism's development. Our defeat was always implicit in the victory of others; our wealth has always generated our poverty by nourishing the prosperity of others—the empires and their native overseers.

~ *Eduardo Galeano in* Open Veins of Latin America

FIVE YEARS AGO, shortly after my first trip to "Occupy" Crawford, TX to confront the person I felt murdered my son Casey, I was invited to Caracas, Venezuela to attend the World Social Forum.

Amazingly, at the time, I really had no idea that the World Social Forum was about socialism and I really didn't know much more about President Hugo Chávez other than he was a very vocal opponent of my opponents: George Bush and the US Empire.

That trip to Caracas was a whirlwind of speeches, meetings, and rallies and I even got to meet with President Chávez at the presidential palace, Miraflores. He showed us some of the places where the US-CIA-backed coup attempt happened in April of 2002—a living "*The Revolution Will Not Be Televised*," with our guide being the "star" of the show. Chávez not only survived that coup attempt because of his people, but also has thrived as the socialist/anti-imperialist president of Venezuela for over 12 years now.

Back in Caracas, I stumbled through my meetings and obligations, just knowing enough to survive that trip. However, after I returned from the trip to Venezuela for that WSF and my meeting with President Chávez, I was met with deep-seated hostility, even from people I had considered on "the Left."

"Cindy, the enemy of your enemy is not your friend."

"Hugo Chávez is an anti-American, communist dictator."

"Blah, blah, blah!" I was even hauled in before Arianna Huffington and thoroughly scolded for my "indiscretion." (A working definition of irony: I have stuck to my "peace at all costs" platform all these years and am nearly broke, yet

Arianna is a political chameleon and just sold her soul—oops I mean website—to AOL for hundreds of millions of dollars).

In the early years of my activism, I did a lot of things that I wasn't ready for—and meeting this "anti-American, communist, dictator" was one of them. Because of the criticism from what barely passes for the "Left" in this country, I started to do a little more research into Venezuelan politics, Hugo Chávez, and the Bolivarian Revolution. What I discovered greatly relieved me! I felt justified in defending and supporting Chávez and his policies.

Since the beginning of 2006, and my trip to Caracas, I have traveled the world and have met people holding societal positions from presidents on down to Empire-induced beggars on the street; I have run an unsuccessful campaign for Congress against a card-carrying member of the oppressor-class here in the US, Nancy Pelosi (I came in 2nd though); I have been arrested many times and harassed because of my beliefs and activities; I have published five books; been nominated for the Nobel Peace Prize; and have been gifted with four fabulous grandchildren—and all of these experiences combined, along with the death of my son in 2004, has brought me to the conclusion that the system we live under in the US, whether one wants to call it "Capitalism," "Crony Capitalism," "Corporatism," "Imperialism," "Oligarchy," or whatever, is a profoundly and incurably diseased system.

For decades, Venezuela suffered under US corporations, the CIA, and "leaders" (native overseers) who were dependent on and supporters of the rape and pillage of their country by the US (kind of like Egypt's Hosni Mubarak, truly a dictator).

The people were strangled by this system and rose up against it many times, and failed, but the soil was being prepared for one to step in and show the people of Venezuela a new way—

an alternative to the stranglehold that US Capitalist-Imperialism had on his country.

So, in 2010, after I became what I like to call an "organic Marxist," writing my own (wo)manifesto in 2009, called: "*Myth America: 20 Greatest Myths of the Robber Class and the Case for Revolution,"* I wanted to go back to Venezuela to chat with Chávez about something more significant than "Señor Peligro" (Mr. Danger) George Bush. I wanted to witness a socialist revolution in process. I wanted to be able to come back to the US with evidence of a better way. To do that, I also felt it was urgent to dispel the "myths" about President Chávez and the Bolivarian Revolution.

I received permission to interview the President and I raised the money to travel there with two camera operators, and our "mission" was to interview the President, and talk to people in the "barrios" of Venezuela to see how this revolution was affecting them—screw the oligarchy and opposition that still remain there. Their sob-stories of their lost wealth (stolen from the people) to the socialist way are told over and over and over and over and over again in Venezuelan media and our media, too. I had no sympathy for the robbers who became a little less wealthy sitting behind their protective walls in their mansions feeling sorry for themselves.

I wish that could happen here in the US—wouldn't it be a shame if Mr. Rockefeller had to have a few of his oil wells and properties expropriated to pay for healthcare, environmental cleanup, jobs, and education for we the people here in the US? No, it wouldn't be a shame—the wealth that someone like a Rockefeller, JP Morgan, Vanderbilt, Rothschild, Gates, Soros, Jobs, Koch, Winfrey, or T. Boone Pickens have accumulated is obscene and belongs to everyone, not just them.

I asked one formerly illiterate and disadvantaged person in the barrio of San Agustin what she thought about the amendment to the Bolivarian Republic's new Constitution (more about the Constitution later) that allows Chávez to run for president without term limits. She said:

"I hope he is President for life, we would die for him and the revolution."

Many people did die during the 2002 coup attempt defending and supporting Chávez.

Chávez loves the people of Venezuela—he owes them his life.

What do we owe to such a person and his country that are being unfairly and unjustly demonized at every opportunity by the Robber Class in our own country? We owe him a balanced look at what he's done, why he's done it, and what he is still attempting to do with all the obstacles in his way from weather patterns to El Imperio.

I had fully intended on producing a movie with this same title, but a not-so-funny thing (sabotage) happened on the way to making it—but that's another story for another time.

This book is my humble attempt at showing appreciation to my supporters and to President Chávez for helping me see that there is a better way to do things than we do them here in the US.

Revolution cannot be achieved or accomplished by one person, no matter how dedicated, smart, or charismatic they are.

Is Chávez's way perfect? I don't think so (and I will examine the challenges, too), but that's the beauty of revolution—it's a continuing process that takes everybody working together to achieve as close to perfection as mere humans are able. I am here in Cuba today—and after five decades, I can attest to the fact that the Cuba revolution is a living, breathing entity. However, sadly, after over five decades of living in the US, I think our initial revolution is dead and it's time for a new, non-violent (this time) one.

Recently, I started to get dozens of messages from friends and supporters panicked because they had heard that the president of Venezuela just died in Cuba! All the media was busy burying Chávez and some were even exulting over his "greatly exaggerated" demise—and most had killed the Revolution, too.

Obviously, Chávez survived and the Revolution continues—but is there a new leader to take his place in the horrible event that something does happen to him? I believe that there are millions of Venezuelans who will not allow the Revolution to die, even if Chávez does.

The Bolivarian Revolution in Venezuela is not an uprising like we have seen in the Arab world and closer to home in Madison, Wisconsin, nor is it a huge campout. No, it is actually a plan, and during our interview in Montevideo, Chávez told me that because of all the "obstacles" and "challenges" they have really only accomplished about 10% of what the Revolution has set out to do. (Does that sound like an autocrat? If he were one, 90% would be accomplished).

The Representative Republic that was formed by the plutocracy in this nation has only led us to increasing fascistic oppressions and a growing income disparity that is the largest in so-called industrialized nations. Chávez is leading a "Great Experiment" in Venezuela at a time when the "Great American Experiment," described by Alexis de Tocqueville, is failing and trying so hard to save itself for the wealthy and power-mad that it attacks small countries and leaders like President Hugo Chávez— because the plutocracy still calls the shots and is terrified of "the threat of a good example."

I want to tell you up front that I love this subject. It is not a non-biased look, but I can promise you it will be an honest look and one that you won't find many other places. I will present statistics and facts that can't be woven around a web of Imperial lies, yet, tinted with enthusiasm and inspiration.

There is a better way—there is a path we can follow to freedom and peace. It won't be easy, but it'll be worth every step we must take.

¡Vamos, Mis amigos!

Chapter One

A Brief History of (some) Time

CONQUISTADORES

BY THE TIME THE FIRST WHITE Europeans sailed to the Americas looking for riches, exploitable land, and slave-able people, there were approximately 100 million indigenous living in the hemisphere. Since no census was operating, or even needed at the time, we don't know for sure—the figure is a guestimate.

After centuries of pillage and murder from the tip of South America to the northern most reaches of the Spanish Empire in California, white Europeans had almost completely colonized, subjugated, and/or destroyed all the native populations they came in contact with.

Those resisting colonialism in Latin America usually took the form of indigenous struggles combined with the help of slaves and free blacks. By the time the American and French Revolutions had been fought, and won, Latin America had become a mix of white Europeans and Native Americans—called "Creoles" —living alongside the colonizers in discontent, for the most part.

The first Caribbean nation to fall under the struggle for independence was Haiti—Haitian rebels had been inspired by the two previously mentioned revolutions in France and the US.

Then, in Central and South America, the dreaded (for imperialists) "Domino Theory" (widely touted to drum up support for the disastrous Vietnam conflict during the '60s—if Vietnam toppled to communism, then the other nations in Asia would soon follow), really began to take place!

With the recent events in the Arab world today, we are seeing a version of this. The uprisings against the dictatorship of Ben Ali in Tunisia gave hope and inspiration to those in Yemen, Iran, Egypt, Iraq, Palestine, etc. We have yet to see the full flowering, nor understand fully, the implications of these dominoes toppling.

Towards the end of the 18th and beginning of the 19th centuries, the people under Spanish colonial rule began to form isolated, yet persistent, forms of resistance against that rule. Like Great Britain, circa the American Revolution, Colonial Spain was feeling the fatigue of holding onto such a far-flung Empire (rather like the US today), and even though the maintenance of this Empire was costly and difficult, the Spanish decided to entrench and send reinforcements when the native people began to itch for independence.

Most of the indigenous rebellions in what are now Venezuela, Ecuador, Bolivia, Panama, and Colombia were easily suppressed by the Spanish working with sympathizers in the Americas who were afraid their way of life would be diminished under independence.

However, there arose a Venezuelan-born man of Spanish descent who had the persistence and vision to lead the above five mentioned countries from colonial rule to independence: Simón José Antonio de la Santísima Trinidad Bolívar y Palacios Ponte y Blanco, commonly known as Simón Bolívar. Bolívar is widely considered the Liberator of Latin America and recognized even here in the US for his leadership and revolutionary struggle.

Indeed, statues and monuments are erected to Bolívar all over the world. The one pictured below is in our own nation's capital: Washington, DC.

Bolívar was only one of the leaders for Latin American independence for the better part of two decades, but he was also the first president of Venezuela and died in self-imposed exile in Panama waiting for a boat to sail to France.

However, Bolívar's vision didn't stop at independence from colonial rule. He dreamed of a united Latin America under a loose federation of states. His vision was remarkable, because no sooner did each state throw off the shackles of its oppressors, a new oppressor was installed: The USA—the nation that Simón Bolívar culled so much inspiration from and admired so deeply. Bolívar held such high esteem for Thomas Jefferson that he sent one of his nephews to be educated at Jefferson's pride and joy: the University of Virginia.

The Ghost of Manhattan and his Doctrine

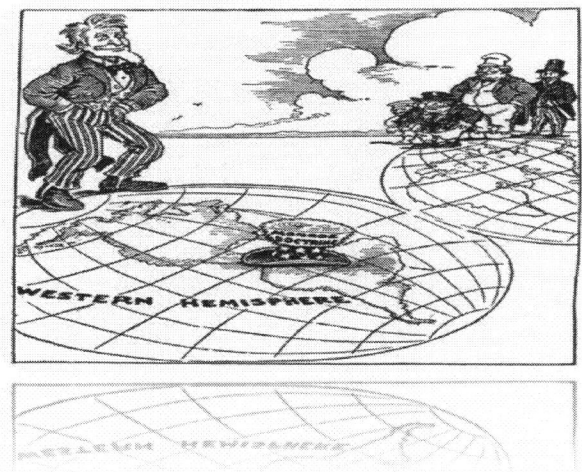

James Monroe, the 5th president of the USA, first introduced his Doctrine on December 2, 1823, as Central and South America were embroiled in struggles for independence. The doctrine simply stated that no other European powers would help Spain to re-colonize Latin America—or colonize her absent Spanish rule. It was a "hands off" doctrine that was chuckled at by ancient, powerful Europe, but met with gratitude by those fighting for independence in Latin America. How could Bolívar even guess that a nation he admired so greatly would actually be interested in complete regional hegemony and not be concerned at all with the people of Latin America?

To delve more deeply into the roots of imperial expansion that took hold on our neighbors to the south "Team Cindy" traveled down to the Hollywood Hills on a beautiful fall day to sit at the feet of legendary intellectual, Gore Vidal, to literally bask in his brilliance.

I wanted to chat with Gore because I (without blowing smoke up anyone's kazoo) think that, besides being one of the leading intellectuals in the US, he is one of the most interesting people that I know.

At his home, on what he calls "Spanish Land," which is a living-US history museum, surrounded by pictures of his father's paramour, Amelia Earhart; one of Gore's best-friends, Johnny Carson; and other famous and infamous figures, I not only learned more about the Monroe Doctrine, but I heard a most fascinating story of an episode in Gore's life when he lived down in Antigua, Guatemala after he was released from active duty as a enlisted reservist on an Army supply ship in the Alaskan Aleutian Islands. Adrift, he told me that he went down to Antigua, Guatemala and purchased a huge Baroque ex-convent for "two grand," where he lived from 1947–1949.

First, the Monroe Doctrine—if every student had a history professor like Gore Vidal, I am sure that history would be learned and not "doomed to be repeated." Gore wove a tale not so much of the Monroe Doctrine itself, where the fledgling Empire just told Europe "hands off our hemisphere," but of the man whom the Doctrine is named for: James Monroe.

"Monroe wasn't terribly interested in politics, or terribly interesting either—in his later life he took to wandering around Manhattan and mothers would frighten their young children by tales of the 'Ghost of Manhattan,' " began Gore. Even though Monroe was kind of a dud, he could "read maps" and see the great potential for, not only other imperial powers settling to a greater degree in the hemisphere, but opportunity for our own expansion.

Gore didn't have too much more to say about the Monroe Doctrine, except that it came at a time of "great chauvinism and corruption," even more than usual. Gore was surprised I was so interested in it, since he opined that if one asked the "average American" about the Doctrine, *"They won't have any idea what you're talking about."* Indeed, with recent Pew polling showing that over 40% of Americans couldn't even name the current vice president, I am sure Gore must be correct about such "ancient history."

"United Fruit Owned Guatemala"

During the years that Gore lived in Guatemala, United Fruit Company owned over 42% of the country and didn't pay a penny in taxes.

United Fruit sounds like a sweet company doesn't it? Who isn't for being "united" and who isn't for "fruit?" Fruit is good for you, isn't it?

Well, United Fruit (UF) had deep roots in the US government and our secret police. John Foster Dulles, who was Eisenhower's Secretary of State, had unethical business connections to UF, as did his brother Allen, who was on the board of UF and Director of the CIA. The Dulles brothers were deeply involved in scandal after scandal in Central and South America—I cringe with disgust every time I am forced to fly in and out of Dulles Airport in Virginia when I travel to DC.

The Boys of Mama Dulles also had their bloody handprints all over the overthrow of democratically elected president, Mohammad Mossadegh of Iran, in 1953 (thus causing the "blowback" we are still feeling today).

In a remarkable coincidence, the man Hillary Clinton sent to Egypt during the 2011 uprising was Frank Wisner, Jr. (employed by Mubarak's DC law firm: Patton Boggs) and the son of CIA operative, Frank Wisner, Sr., who was tapped to lead the operation in Guatemala to remove another democratically elected president with socialist leanings like Mossadegh of Iran, Jacobo Arbenz in 1954.

The crime of Arbenz? Taking about one million acres of land from United Fruit (that they weren't using, anyway) to give to Guatemalan peasants to cultivate. Did Arbenz "steal" the land from United Fruit? No—in 1936, Dictator Jorge Ubico had leased the land to UF for 99 years with the stipulation that UF would never have to pay taxes. Arbenz was even willing to pay UF for the land that the people of Guatemala owned anyway. He was willing to pay the tax dodgers the same value that UF claimed on their US income taxes. Even though "expropriating" the property of the people was never even discussed or proposed, the evil Dulles brothers and Eisenhower went on a propaganda smear campaign manufacturing ties between Arbenz and Moscow.

When Gore Vidal was living in Antigua, besides writing the groundbreaking and super-controversial: *The City and the Pillar,* he had a regular visitor, the president of Guatemala's parliament under the presidency of the predecessor of Arbenz, Juan-Jose Arevalo (also a member of the Revolutionary Action Party)—Mario Monteforte Toledo. Toledo had a woman in the town—"very scandalous" Gore said with a twinkle in his eye. Even though Gore is one of America's leading intellectuals, he also loves scandals.

According to Gore, at the end of his term, Arevalo had to beat a hasty retreat from Guatemala and go back into exile in Argentina because he had the nerve to think that the only resource in Guatemala, bananas, belonged to the people of Guatemala and that United Fruit should pay their fair share of taxes (similar to Hugo Chávez and oil).

On one such visit Gore was telling Toledo that he may want to "build a wing" to the convent. Gore recounts that Toledo told him that it wouldn't be such a great idea to invest further in the country. Toledo told Gore that the time was getting close when the US was going to "take over" Guatemala for United Fruit.

Gore said: *"Why would the US do that? We just overthrew fascism and evil in the world. (Or so I thought at the time.) Why would we want to be involved in this tiny Central American country? It makes no sense."* Toledo agreed that it seemed crazy, but reassured Gore that a US-CIA-sponsored coup was in the wings because Guatemala was "becoming too successful." Toledo was right, of course. In 1954, the Evil Brothers, heady from their success in Iran overthrowing (by mostly covert means) a democratically elected president, helped United Fruit in overthrowing Jacobo Arbenz.

Gore called the overthrow of Arbenz one of the *"lowest points of the American republic, not that there have been many high points."*

Since the ouster of Arbenz, there has been one dictatorship after the other, *"torture is a way of life"* and Guatemala can now be counted as one of the client states of the US.

Why do I tell this story? Because when I asked Gore to reflect on Venezuela and the way the Empire is simultaneously taunting and demonizing Hugo Chávez as a dictator and a "commie," Gore just said— *"For the oil and for the fact that*

Americans like to make their guns go, 'bang-bang,' it's déjà vu all over again," down in Venezuela, and indeed in many so-called Banana Republics that the slimy hands of the Empire have peeled.

Like Jacobo Arbenz in '50s Guatemala and Hugo Chávez in today's Venezuela, the US cannot stand the *"threat of a good example."*

Because of the Monroe Doctrine and the Roosevelt Corollary to the Monroe Doctrine—which takes Monroe a step further, saying that if ANY US interest is compromised, the US has the right to intervene— there is scarcely a country in Latin America that hasn't felt some kind of US meddling.

LIST OF LATIN AMERICAN COUNTRIES INTERVENED BY THE UNITED STATES:

Argentina, Chile, Haiti, Cuba, Venezuela, Honduras,

Ecuador, Guatemala, Puerto Rico, Nicaragua, Panama,

Dominican Republic, Mexico, El Salvador, Uruguay, Bolivia,

Columbia, Grenada, Costa Rica

Military coup d'état of Salvador Allende in Chile

I hope Gore's story and the long list of countries that the US has stuck its greedy big nose in convinces you that Chávez truly has something to worry about! If he's not constantly worrying about assassination or CIA-backed coups (one of which he survived already—more later), he has to worry about the millions of dollars the US pumps into Venezuela to undermine and destabilize his administration.

To put the cherry on the sundae of US interventionism in Latin America, President Obama's new budget contains funding to aid the political opponents to President Chávez and his party—according to our friend, Eva Golinger:

The US government is setting the terrain for the 2012 presidential elections in Venezuela, soliciting funding to back anti-Chávez groups and help prepare a "candidate" to oppose Chávez. Republicans call for an "embargo" against the oil-producing nation.

This week, US President Barack Obama presented Congress with a $3.7 trillion dollar budget for 2012, the most expensive budget in United States history. Within his massive request, which proposes cuts in important social programs and federal jobs throughout the country, is a partition for special funding for anti-Chávez groups in Venezuela.

Included in the whopping $3.7 trillion request is over $670 billion for the Pentagon's ever-increasing annual budget, nearly $75 billion for the intelligence community, and $55.7 billion for the State Department and the US Agency for International Development (USAID).

For the first time in recent history, the Foreign Operations Budget (State Department) openly details direct funding of at least $5 million to anti-Chávez groups in Venezuela. Specifically, the budget justification document states, "These funds will help strengthen and support a Venezuelan civil society that will protect democratic space and seek to serve the interests and needs of the Venezuelan people. Funding will enhance citizens' access to objective information, facilitate peaceful debate on key issues, provide support to democratic institutions and processes, promote citizen participation, and encourage democratic leadership."

Isn't that special? Mr. Preznit-Change-O has deviated little from the trajectory of the Bush regime, but none so obvious as US meddling in the internal affairs of sovereign Venezuela.

Why?

Because Chávez, like Bolívar long before him, not only dreams of a united Latin America, but is showing the way.

What would it be like here in the US if instead of propagandized, we were educated?

What would it be like here if we were guaranteed basic human rights instead of groveling for crumbs off of the master's table?

What would it be like if the wealth and resources of this country were more equitably distributed, and the wealth that has been stolen from us for generations was given back?

Better, that's what!

What is the major obstacle to such a Bolivarian Revolution happening here in the US?

Ignorance.

Let's take care of that...

The United Fruit Company

Pablo Naruda

*When the trumpet sounded
everything was prepared on earth,
and Jehovah gave the world
to Coca-Cola Inc., Anaconda,*

Ford Motors, and other corporations.
The United Fruit Company
reserved for itself the most juicy
piece, the central coast of my world,
the delicate waist of America.

It rebaptized these countries
Banana Republics,
and over the sleeping dead,
over the unquiet heroes
who won greatness,
liberty, and banners,
it established an opera buffa:
it abolished free will,
gave out imperial crowns,
encouraged envy, attracted
the dictatorship of flies:
Trujillo flies, Tachos flies
Carias flies, Martinez flies,
Ubico flies, flies sticky with
submissive blood and marmalade,
drunken flies that buzz over
the tombs of the people,
circus flies, wise flies
expert at tyranny.

With the bloodthirsty flies
came the Fruit Company,
amassed coffee and fruit
in ships which put to sea like
overloaded trays with the treasures
from our sunken lands.

Meanwhile the Indians fall
into the sugared depths of the
harbors and are buried in the
morning mists;
a corpse rolls, a thing without
name, a discarded number,

a bunch of rotten fruit
thrown on the garbage heap.

Post-script to this chapter:

Since my son Casey was killed in Iraq, I have embarked on many campaigns to change...myself.

I got rid of my car; I am a war-tax resister; and I have continued my vegetarianism.

After doing the research for this chapter, I started to loathe myself for eating bananas from Dole or Chiquita. It is hard to find free-trade bananas in my town.

Formerly, I ate at least one banana per day, for potassium and other wonderful nutrients available in the little "vitamin in a peel." One day, after I ate a banana with guilt, my mouth started to burn and my gums started to swell. I thought it was odd, but thought maybe something weird was on the peel, or on my hands.

Then, the next day after I ate my banana, the same thing happened—I tried one more time, and the same thing happened.

I researched "allergies to bananas" on the Internet, and an onset of this allergy is not uncommon, but now I will always wonder if my conscience talked my body into rejecting this "bloody" fruit?

Chapter Two

I've got your "ism"

"*Are you now, or have you ever been a member of the Communist Party.*"

~ *Senator Joseph McCarthy*
During the Communist Witch Hunts of the 1950s

AFTER THE APPARENT VICTORY OF THE US and its allies during World War II, many people happily, yet mistakenly, greeted a world free from war, fascism, and tyranny.

How could a world be "free from war" though?

Since the beginning of time there has been profit to be made from war, and after a war that killed millions but made billions, the war profiteers could not imagine a world free from war—that would *NOT* be acceptable to them.

Where was the next "enemy" to come from? A perfect solution was found in "communism." Although the Soviet Union and China were the leading Communist states, communism in and of itself, as an ideology, was a far superior "enemy" than a nation with borders and armies with uniforms and chains of command that could see a precise beginning and finite end to wars.

Essentially, from 1945, an anti-Communist frenzy settled over the "Land of the Free." You know where I am talking about—this "free" Capitalist state, where being a member of the Communist Party should not only have been tolerated, but also fiercely protected.

However, J. Edgar Hoover, under the presidencies of Truman and Eisenhower, was given free rein in pursuing suspected Communists by using illegal means like wire-tapping and burglary. Of course we all know that these Witch Hunts ruined many careers and lives.

I think this is one of the reasons that it is so easy for the global ruling-class to demonize President Hugo Chávez of Venezuela with the tag "Communist." This anti-Communist delusion still permeates American society, today—indeed, one of the names that people have been slinging in my direction since I started my crusade for peace after my son was killed is "communist."

Frequently I respond to these attacks by asking people what they think they mean when they call me communist—not one of them has returned with: "You support an economic system which is the ultimate goal of socialism; where everyone's needs supersede exploitation purely for profit." No, if anyone does answer, they answer with: "Someone who hates America."

Well, if "America" stands for spying, war, killing for profit, torture, environmental destruction, and supporting corporations over citizens, and if I hate these things, then by those people's definition, "Hell, yes," I am a "communist."

Most Americans have no earthly idea about the three relevant terms we want to explore in this chapter: "Capitalism, Socialism, and Communism."

For this book, I could have just looked up definitions for the words: Capitalism, Communism, and Socialism, but since this project began as a documentary, I thought just putting up words on the screen would be pretty boring. Intending to make a documentary that wasn't boring, but fascinating, I decided to ask Professor Angela Davis to enlighten us about the systems.

Let's start with the unknown—the boogie man—the evil monkey in your closet—the "Red under Your Bed"—

Communism

"Communism is the riddle of history solved, and it knows itself to be this solution."

~ *Marx, Private Property and Communism (1844)*

To most people living in the US, this term is just flat out frightening—a certain filmmaker from Michigan even produced an entire film about Capitalism and not even once did the word "Communism" come out of his mouth during the narration.

I want to tell a story that I told in my other e-book, *Myth America,* because it is so relevant here.

During the baby-boom craze (which was also during the "Red Scare" craziness), I had a teacher in my 2nd grade elementary school in Bellflower, CA that I now realize was abusive and nuts.

One day, and I remember this clearly, she asked my combination class of 2nd and 3rd graders a very abusive question.

"If a Red-Communist came up to you and put a gun to your head and told you not to recite the Pledge of Allegiance, what would you do?"

Well, believe it or not, I was a very shy and timid child, but I had the courage of the confidence in my answer, and my hand shot up almost automatically!

"Yes, Cindy Miller" (there were two Cindys in my class), my teacher chose me a little surprised at my eagerness, "what would you do?"

"I wouldn't say it," I crowed, very proud of myself!

Well guess what? That answer was WRONG! And I was made to stand in the corner for being a very bad little American. Who knew?

After the US tried to overthrow the revolutionary government in Cuba á la Bay of Pigs and Operation Mongoose, the USSR and Cuba started to build bases on Cuban soil for the protection of Cuba—from its ugly neighbor immediately to the north. The potential placement of missiles in Cuba was also in reaction to the ICBMs missiles the US had deployed in Italy and Turkey.

I barely remember the details of the Cuban Missile Crisis in1962, but I do remember it—I remember how frightened and uncertain the adults seemed—and when one is five years old, we need our adults to be brave and confident. Years later, learning about how our nation came to the brink of nuclear war, because Cuba was going to allow the USSR to place nuclear missiles on its soil, the way this nation acted about communism began to make sense—but guess what? Again, the propaganda rarely matched the reality.

The USSR is one of the examples that anti-Communists or anti-Socialists like to bandy about as if Stalinism has any relation to Marxism. Stalinism is to Marxism as the US bombing innocent countries into submission is to "freedom."

Calling the military-totalitarian state of the USSR an example of socialism or communism is EXACTLY like the rightwing calling Obama a "Socialist." Any time I see that false accusation flying around I say: *"How DARE you paint socialism with such a corporate-fascist brush!"*

According to Angela Davis, who said during our interview with her: *"I wish Obama was a Socialist,"* communism is not men in black trench coats and hats lurking around threatening our young children with execution if they recite the Pledge of Allegiance. It's simply the ultimate state of socialism.

Whereas socialism can be defined as: "From each according to their ability and to each according to their works," communism makes the final step to societal peace and well-being, in my humble opinion.

Communism: "From each according to their ability and to each according to their NEEDS."

Socialism

The meaning of peace is the absence of opposition to socialism.
~ Karl
Marx

In my travels, debates, and studies, I have found that there are almost as many "socialisms" as there are Socialists!

Marxism, Libertarian Socialism, Mutualism, Syndicalism, Democratic Socialism, Market Socialism, Utopian Socialism, Social Anarchism, Revolutionary Socialism, Eco-Socialism, Scientific Socialism, Socialism of the 21st century—plus everything in between and more! For a more in-depth explanation of all of these different socialist ideologies, I suggest you do some further investigation.

However, it seems that the common thread that binds all of these theories together is the primary belief that the needs of humans should supersede the needs of capital—or profit.

According to Professor Angela Davis, socialism is a system that is NOT based on the "production of profit," but on "fulfilling people's needs."

Under a socialist government, there would be no sense to profit off of delivering such human rights as healthcare, education, and housing, therefore it would either be free or greatly subsidized.

Right here, right now, before we go on to the evolution of Revolution in Venezuela, let's talk about what the Bolivarian Revolution has done just for the people of Venezuela. Compared to the good old USA, in reality, our only choices are between "paper and plastic," "smoking or non-smoking," and "regular or decaffeinated."

During 10 years of Revolution, the Bolivarian Government has been breaking free from paradigms, beating obstacles, exceeding all expectations, facing empires, revolutionizing consciousness, beating foreign and internal propaganda, and even more, defending, as the engine and fuel of the revolutionary project, the deep conviction that the human being is the center and principle of society.

~ Hector

These are some of the achievements of the socialist "experiment" in Venezuela, usually from 1998 to the present day.

- Extreme poverty has fallen from 42% to 9.5%.
- General poverty reduced from 50.5% to 33.4%.
- GINI coefficient has RISEN from .4099 to .4865.
- 96% of the country was literate in 1998.
- 99.6% of the population over 15 is now literate compared to blank percent in 1998.
- Currently VZ spends 7% of its GDP on education compared to 3.9% in 1998. The US? 5.7%
- Today, VZ spends 4.2% of its GDP on healthcare.
- In 1990, childhood (under 5) mortality rate was 25.8%, today it is 13.7%
- Unemployment has dropped from 12% in 1998 to 6.1 percent in 2009.
- In May 2007, the minimum wage in VZ became the highest in Latin America.
- Workers receive a bonus (US$139) above their wages every month for food.
- Pensions have been increased to the minimum wage.
- From 1998, VZ food production has increased by 24%.
- The public debt dropped from 73.5% of the GDP in 1998 to 14.4% of GDP (one of the lowest deficits in the world). The public debt as percentage of the GDP here in this debtor nation? 58.90%!
- Infocentros (Information Centers) give the public access to info and communication technologies.

- Women head 4/5 of the Public Powers and women's presence in the National Assembly has increased from 10% to 16.5%.
- As a country involved in ZERO (according to Venezuelan Assistant Foreign Minister, Temir Porras) wars, Venezuela spends only 1.4% of its GDP on the military. Compared to 4.3% for its imperialistic neighbor to the north.

ALARMING STATS ON POVERTY IN THE USA (ACCORDING TO WORLDHUNGER.ORG)

Poverty in the United States

- In 2009, 43.6 million people were poor, up from 39.8 million in 2008 and 37.3 million in 2007. The nation's official poverty rate in 2009 was 14.3%, up from 13.2% in 2008—the second statistically significant annual increase in the poverty rate since 2004. (Census Bureau 2010a p.13)

- The poverty rate in 2009 was the highest since 1994, but was 8.1 percentage points lower than the poverty rate in 1959, the first year for which poverty estimates are available. The number of people in poverty in 2009 is the largest number in the 51 years for which poverty estimates are available. (Census Bureau 2010a p.13)

- Between 2008 and 2009, the poverty rate increased for children under the age of 18 from 19.0% to 20.7%. Thus one in five children in the United States lives in poverty. Almost half of these children (9.3%) live in extreme poverty. (Census Bureau 2010a p.13)

- In 2009, the family poverty rate and the number of families in poverty were 11.1% and 8.8 million, respectively, up from 10.3% and 8.1 million in 2008. (Census Bureau 2010a p.18)

- 19 million Americans (6.3%) live in extreme poverty. This means their family's cash income is less than half of the poverty line, or less than about $11,000 a year for a family of four. (Census Bureau 2010a p.19)

- 16 million low-income households either paid more for rent and utilities than the federal government says is affordable, or lived in overcrowded or substandard housing (CBPP 2007).

- The percentage of people without health insurance increased to 16.7% in 2009 from 15.4% in 2008. The number of uninsured people increased to 50.7 million in 2009 from 46.3 million in 2008 (Census Bureau 2010a p. 22)

Again—why is Chávez and his work so demonized and vilified in our press and international press?

Repeat after me: The Threat of a Good Example.

CAPITALISM

"I have said it already: I am convinced that the way to build a new and better world is not capitalism. Capitalism leads us straight to hell."
~ Hugo Chávez

First of all, what do you think of when you see or hear the word, "capitalism?"

Back in my ill-informed days, I would have thought of "a chicken in every pot and a car in every garage." Certain buzzwords would have easily sprung to my mind, like "democracy," "prosperity," "security," "patriotism," etc. Even though I was a member of the poor working-class, I thought I was in the middle-class and, I thought, even though things might not be good right now, "good times" are just around the corner.

Now when I think of "capitalism," I think of "war," "exploitation," "pillage," "plunder," "slavery," "debt," "poverty," and the scourge of the "haves and have mores."

Professor Angela Davis defined capitalism as, *"The economic system that is based on production of profit at the expense of workers who actually produce the goods."* Professor Davis went on to explain that capitalism's greatest trick is to fool people into believing that workers actually get paid for what they produce when, in reality, they are getting paid for their "capacity and ability to work."

Profit is the "nature of capitalistic exploitation" because capital exploits people who have nothing to sell but their labor.

Most of us know that many of the good, union manufacturing jobs that were the back-bone of the working-class after World War II, have been slowly, but surely, exported out of the country to third-world nations where workers are paid as little as $3 per day to construct the cheap consumer goods that return to the US to stock the shelves of such places as Wal-Mart, where workers have to oftentimes avail themselves of social services to survive.

This is one of the more egregious examples of turning humans into virtual slaves to make an even greater profit-margin for capital—we recently learned that some federal prisoners are being paid 23 cents an hour to build parts for Patriot missiles that sell on the world-wide arms racket for $5.3 million each! Wow! Is anyone surprised that the war machine will not pay a living wage to make its products that are only built for destruction?

We have been "treated" to so many advantages to being a member of the exploited class over the last two years!

First there was the bankster bailout towards the end of 2008, which both US political parties (including Obama and Nancy Pelosi) supported and rammed down our throats, while doing nothing to stop the foreclosure and eviction hemorrhage that was hurting millions more people than those on Wall Street who actually caused the crisis.

Then in the middle of 2010, an oil well leased by British Petroleum exploded and gushed millions of gallons of oil for months in the Gulf of Mexico. Was BP punished and its profits confiscated for the good of the commons, environment, and people who were killed, injured or made ill by this disaster? No, BP was asked to put $20 billion into an escrow account that was then administered by a Kenneth R. Feinberg (who has administered many such escrow accounts) whose firm makes a "flat fee" of $1.25 million dollars a month to manage it.

The ringmasters of our political circus are these oil companies and it seems like everything the government does is to protect them and help them increase profit at the expense of workers AND the planet.

In a revolutionary socialist government, BP would have been under the democratic control of the workers, and I think the workers would have insisted upon that acoustic switch—that according to an April 29, 2010 article in the *Wall Street Journal* could have been a "third line of defense" that may have stopped millions of gallons of crude oil from spilling into the gulf, killing people and wildlife—and the effects are still being felt. The switch would have cost a paltry $500,000 and would have saved lives and money.

As I write this book, life on this planet has, once again, reached a crisis due to unbridled capitalism and one of its evil spawns, neo-liberalism. In March, a 9.0 earthquake occurred in Japan, causing a huge tsunami that flooded the Fukushima Daichi nuclear power plant, which has been in meltdown ever since. Not only is the radiation about one million times more than acceptable, but also Japan relies heavily on nuclear power for its energy needs.

Around the time of the anniversaries of the a-bombs that were unleashed on civilian populations in Hiroshima and Nagasaki, I was invited to Japan to work to abolish nuclear power in Japan and the situation there is dire.

Why did anybody ever think it was even a remotely good idea to build nuclear power plants in the Ring of Fire? The Robber Class has built those reactors on fault lines in my state of California; but now in Japan, the worst-case scenario is unfolding before the world's horrified eyes!

Recently, it was revealed that after this nuclear cataclysm in Japan, President Chávez is holding off on further development of a nuclear power plant in Venezuela that was being planned in collaboration with the Russians.

President Chávez wisely stated: *"For now, I have ordered the freezing of the plans we have been developing ... for a peaceful nuclear program."* He went on, *"I do not have the least doubt that this (the potential for a nuclear catastrophe in Japan) is going to alter in a very strong way the plans to develop nuclear energy in the world."* I, for one, am thrilled that Venezuela is rethinking a program that I was not too happy with from the beginning.

What did the "leader of the free world" have to think about the nuclear catastrophe post-earthquake and tsunami? Well, we are pressing ahead with our nuclear plans—of course. Not even two months after the unimaginable disaster in Japan, Obama announced more than $8 billion dollars in federal loan guarantees to build the first nuclear power plant in the US in over three decades. Contrary to all evidence, Obama claims that nuclear power is not only necessary, but safe.

It seems to me that in this system of capitalism, there is no risk that exists that is too great for capital to take—if we are the ones that are exposed to that risk.

Capitalism does not mean freedom—as I have demonstrated, it means exploitation for profit. There are thousands of examples throughout history of this—but it's time to move on to the next system that I want to explore.

Capitalism means slavery to most of us—and the really sad thing is—most of us don't even realize it!

NOTABLE SOCIALISTS OR ADVOCATES OF SOCIALISM

(USA)

ALBERT EINSTEIN, SUSAN B. ANTHONY, HELEN KELLER,

EUGENE V. DEBS, FRANCIS BELLAMY
(AUTHOR OF THE ORIGINAL PLEDGE OF ALLEGIANCE),

ED ASNER, HUGO CHÁVEZ, NOAM CHOMSKY,

MARTIN LUTHER KING, JR, DR. BENJAMIN SPOCK,

SENATOR BERNIE SANDERS OF VERMONT, DOROTHY DAY,

HENRY DAVID THOREAU, SEAN PENN, MOTHER JONES,

ANGELA DAVIS, CINDY SHEEHAN

Chapter 3

The Seeds of Revolution

JUST LIKE "SOCIALISM," THE WORD, "REVOLUTION," here in the US, is another super-scary word, unless we are talking about a "Chevy Revolution" or the "Pancake Revolution" at IHOP.

It seems in this capitalist society, the world "Revolution," can be used only in advertising slogans to be acceptable.

In some circles, the only "acceptable" revolution is one that began in 1776 and ended in 1783 with the Treaty of Paris.

For example:

Russian Revolution = Bad

Cuban Revolution = Very Bad

US Revolution = Justified and Righteous

Revolution is literally an orbital motion around a point—like the earth traveling in its orbit over and over and over—so, it's strange that the overthrow of a system or government, by a people committed to complete change, is called a "Revolution," but it is. Usually, the rebels want a 180-degree change from the old ways.

However, in this context, revolution has come to denote when a people get tired of being mis-ruled by tyrants, despots, dictators, or kings and organize in some fashion to overthrow that rule.

It is a basic human right to be governed properly that has been enshrined in our own Constitution, and when "In the course of human events," governments no longer work for the people, the people have the existential right to revolt.

In the '80s and '90s, Venezuela was in a place where its own oil-garchy, US oil companies, the World Bank, and the IMF were calling the shots and the income disparity between the rich and poor was growing in an alarming fashion.

Most everyone knows that Venezuela is an oil rich country, but for most of its history, most Venezuelans were still illiterate and living below the poverty line—the people were appropriately restless and hopeless, until a revolutionary moment happened (more about that in the next chapter) and a movement began to arise in the civil society and in the military—and from these moments, a leader arose.

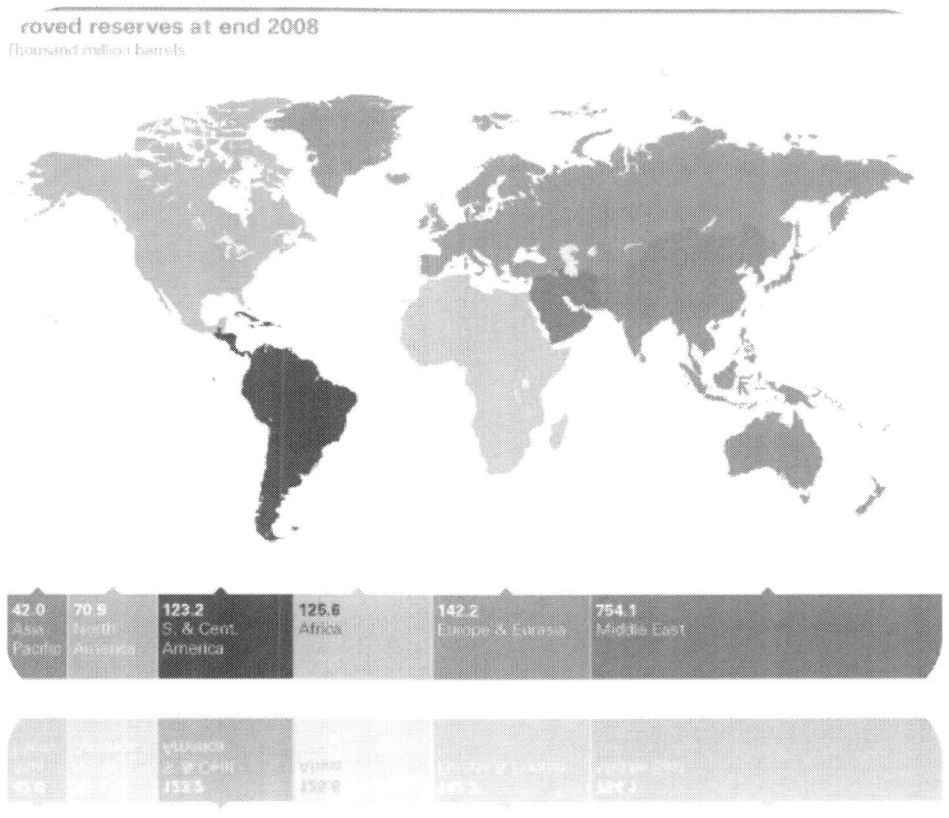

BP's Updated World Proved Oil Reserves Map ~ June 11, 2009

Enter: Hugo Chávez Frias (stage far left)

> *"I think that from the time I left the academy I was oriented toward a revolutionary movement. . . . The Hugo Chávez who entered there was a kid from the hills, a llanero with aspirations of playing professional baseball. Four years later, a second lieutenant came out who had taken the revolutionary path. Someone who didn't have obligations to anyone, who didn't belong to any movement, who was not enrolled in any party, but who knew very well where I was headed."*
>
> *~ Hugo Chávez*

Hugo Chávez Frias, most commonly known as Hugo Chávez, was born on July 28,1954 in Sabaneta, in Western Venezuela, to two teachers.

Chávez's story is truly a log cabin tale. He was born in a mud hut to an impoverished family of Amerindian, Afro-Venezuelan, and Spanish descent.

I don't want to go too much into Chávez's early life—except to say that his experiences growing up poor, with six brothers, to two hard-working school teacher parents influenced him greatly.

Hugo and his older brother, Adan, lived with their grandmother Rosa because their family was so poor. All of this information is readily available in numerous other sources.

Chávez's love for baseball (popular in Venezuela) is also well known (many USAians love baseball, too). He loved to play the sport and girls occupied his thoughts as he grew older—normal stuff. It's kind of strange that we do know so much about President Chávez's life and not so much about Barack Obama's. Hmm?

As someone who grew up (in relative terms) poor in the US, I know the poverty and struggles of Chávez are what gave him his compassion for the poor people of Venezuela and, as a leader, truly sprung from the working class and is one of us. The elitists that sit at the top of the food chain here in the US have no stinking idea what we go through here in the working and poor classes and what's more they don't really give a crap, either.

One thing that causes me pause about Hugo Chávez's early life is that he took so well to the military academy and military life and indeed was one of the leaders of a military coup attempt against a sitting president of Venezuela—but I am convinced that he was inspired by leftist Latin Americans before him, like the President of Peru, Juan Velasco Alvarado, who felt that the military must be in service to the working class when the ruling class overstepped its boundaries; and like Omar Torrijos who inspired Chávez by his peasant land reform act in Panama.

There is much evidence that US interests assassinated Torrijos. Notables, such as former Panamanian military dictator, Manuel Noriega, and economic hit man, John Perkins, both present evidence that the CIA planted a bomb in Torrijos' airplane that exploded, killing him in 1982.

Besides meeting Velasco and Torrijos and being inspired by their work, Chávez read widely from Che Guevara, Marx, and Napoleon Bonaparte. Through his studies, his experiences, and his fundamental opposition to the butcher in Chile, Agosto Pinochet, by the time he was 21 or 22, he became convinced that Venezuela needed a "leftist" government.

Now all of the above facts are things that anyone can read about, but I want to share a few things that I have observed in my limited time spent with world leaders.

The first president that I ever met was George Bush—his handshake was extremely weak, his eyes were eerily vacant, and his aura was stiff and ice cold. When my family met with him shortly after our Casey was killed, we all got the creepiest feelings. My other children, Casey's father, and I all came from that meeting up at Ft. Irwin, Washington, with a great feeling of confusion and guilt. We were confused because we still can't figure out why we were invited to meet with this man when he was going to only mouth empty platitudes and insincere "condolences," and we also felt guilty because we weren't more vocal about our opposition to him—although we did voice our budding concerns.

The first presidential wannabe that I met was Senator John McCain—the first time we met was when he was the warm up act for George Bush at Ft. Irwin. There, he was personable and reasonable—not like the John McCain I came to know better after Camp Casey who basically called me a "liar" for recounting some EXACT conversations that we had, especially one on Inauguration Day in 2005. I had traveled to DC to protest Bush's second term and McCain and I ran into each other on the set of *Good Morning America* where we were both guests. I reintroduced myself and told him I was protesting the war that killed my son and he said: *"Keep it up, we need to hear your voice."* After Camp Casey he denied it telling me: *"Why would I ever say that? I support the wars."*

Beats me, McCain, but you said it—why would I say you said it, if you didn't?

The second presidential desperate wannabe that I met along the way was then Senator Hillary Clinton, who was even colder than Bush and after I and another Gold Star Mother, Lynn Bradach, poured our hearts out to her she told the press: *"We have to stay in Iraq to honor the sacrifices of their sons,"* which was the exact opposite of what we told her. Since that day, I was a strong opponent of Clinton and some people in New York State even wanted me to move there and run against her! What a She-Bush!

The third person I met was a presidential going-to-be: Barack Obama. It's funny that I don't really remember much about the meeting except that he insisted that none of his aides, or my colleagues, or any press would be in the meeting. Then I remember him berating me for being casually dressed (I was on a peace caravan at the time), and I don't remember much after that. I just know he said a lot without really saying much and didn't want ANYTHING to be on the record. I angrily wrote about my meetings with Hillary and McWarMonger, but I don't remember even being asked about that meeting. There wasn't even one member of the press waiting for me when I emerged from his office. Hmm...?

So, after these experiences with politicians of the Empire, I went to Venezuela. As I mentioned before, I wasn't sure what to expect out of a meeting with Chávez, but I was very pleasantly surprised. I met a person of warmth and compassion who is just like me and can't talk to a person without touching them (not in inappropriate ways). Chávez's persona is not drugged-out distant like Bush's; sniveling coward-like war criminal, McCain; cold-cut stone like Hillary's; nor weaselly evasive like Barack Obama's.

Chávez may not be 100% polished, but he is a real person who says real things and is not 1000% fake like most of our politicians.

I have seen him stride confidently into large crowds with nothing between him and them besides his clothes. And these are outdoor crowds that haven't gone through several layers of rigid security and/or background checks to be admitted to an Imperial event with The One. I imagine Chávez's minimal security detail (not like the armored convoys our presidents travel in—because they are not so much loved) has fits when he does this, but the working and poor classes in Latin America adore him, for the most part.

I have been worried about his security when I have had the opportunity to be present with him—and by proximity, my security, too. Chávez is just that open and available, and I think he would be miserable if he had to sequester himself from the public like most world leaders are forced to do—for example, when layers of police state militaristic forces protect the attendees at G8 or G20 summits from protesters who have their rights to protest taken from them because a bunch of rich jackals decided to gather in one place to figure out how to rob us better.

Commandante Fidel Castro, one of the leaders of the Cuban Revolution in 1959 (one of the "bad" revolutions) that overthrew US-backed Cuban dictator, Fulgencio Batista, has been another friend and inspiration for Hugo Chávez. Whereas the Castros and Guevaras mostly gave birth (after a lot of persistence, failure, and pain) to the Cuban Revolution, the budding unrest in Venezuela gave birth to Hugo Chávez as a revolutionary leader.

I have had the immense privilege to visit Cuba twice now—(Note: I am revising this chapter from Havana, right now, my 3rd time) and if more USAians could go down there and see the beautiful country that has withstood the bullying from the north and feel the warmth of Cubans, they would see that there was never really anything to fear. Castro and the Revolution just want what's best for *their* nation and wrested it free from the control and dominance of US companies and the mob.

Cuba for Cubans—wow, just like Venezuela for the Venezuelans and Libya for the Libyans. What a concept!

Anyway, back to our hero. When Chávez was a young military officer, the conditions were ripe in Venezuela for an uprising.

In 1989, political conditions in Venezuela were very much like the US today—there were only two political parties, which does not make for much of a "democracy" anywhere. A propagandistic media, the oligarchy, and the International Monetary Fund (IMF) also controlled the nation.

In 1989, one of the candidates for one of the only two aforementioned political parties (Democratic Action), Carlos Andres Perez (CAP) ran for president of Venezuela on a platform promising the people that he would not send Venezuela further into debt with the IMF, using the very populist sounding rhetoric that the IMF is a "neutron bomb that killed people but left the buildings standing." He also said that the World Bank economists were "genocide workers in the pay of economic totalitarianism."

However, as in the tradition of most politicians, shortly after his victory and inauguration, CAP reneged on his campaign promise and signed onto the IMF for a $4.5 billion dollar loan to Venezuela in a plan known as the *Washington Consensus*.

The Washington Consensus began as a narrow plan to "fix" the economic and social crises in South America during the 1970s and expanded during the 1980s. The Washington Consensus came to a crescendo during the time of CAP and his ill-fated foray into IMF debt-slavery.

When the IMF and private banking cartels loan money to developing nations (like the $4.5 billion to Venezuela in 1989), it always comes with harsh conditions so that the loans will be repaid and the poor of each country can become poorer.

Most of the time "adjustment measures" are imposed on the people of a country so the governments can receive the loans, such as: raising taxes, raising tariffs (and prices), devaluation of the currency, and reducing government expenditures. Not so surprisingly, many governments go into a default situation on these loans as their countries became poorer and poorer.

Because of these stringent conditions and the resultant growing gap between the rich and the poor, many activists have organized protests at IMF, World Bank, and World Trade Organization (WTO) gatherings.

The failure of the Washington Consensus to succeed at this globalization (i.e., Venezuela paying off its debt during the Chávez administration), the wealthy nations have gone to the G8 and G20 formats with former Great Britain Prime Minister claiming after the last G20 summit in London (during which there were massive protests), "the old Washington Consensus is over."

To be fair to the person credited the most with formulating the Washington Consensus—which even he agrees was a very nasty name—John Williamson had hoped that the loans to these developing countries would be used to rebuild infrastructure and create jobs—not be sucked into a crooked bureaucratic wasteland where much of this money was given to

US corporations to build large projects that ended up costing indigenous populations even more money—such as dams and other large civil projects.

Neo-liberalism reared its butt-ugly head here in the US at the end of 2008, when the banking system almost collapsed, but due to the quick thinking of the Congress that bailed out the banks, to the detriment of the already cash-strapped citizens, a few banks and investment houses such as Lehman Brothers and Merrill Lynch collapsed, but everybody's "favorite," Goldman Sachs, grew stronger.

Neo-liberalism, in general, and the Washington Consensus, in particular, simply mean: *Privatized profits and socialized losses.*

As Nobel Economics Prize winner Joseph Stiglitz said about neo-liberalism shortly before the banking crisis:

> *The world has not been kind to neo-liberalism, that grab bag of ideas based on the fundamentalist notion that markets are self-correcting, allocate resources efficiently, and serve the public interest well. It was this market*

fundamentalism that underlay Thatcherism, Reaganomics, and the so-called "Washington Consensus" in favor of privatization, liberalization, and independent central banks focusing single-mindedly on inflation.

Neo-liberal market fundamentalism was always a political doctrine serving certain interests. It was never supported by economic theory. Nor, it should now be clear, is it supported by historical experience. Learning this lesson may be the silver lining in the cloud now hanging over the global economy.

I highly doubt that the globalists needed to learn anything—the crisis and risks only belong to the people, not the elites. I am sure most of the people in Venezuela, being illiterate and ill-informed due to the education system (which charged a fee for many students to even attend), hadn't heard of neo-liberalism, the Washington Consensus, or John Williamson—what they did know was that CAP broke a promise and prices were rising and the subsidy for fuel, that they had counted on to help make ends meet, was going down.

Oftentimes when discontent is brewing, flashpoints are required to bring about a full-fledged rebellion—the Boston Massacre comes to mind.

On February 27, 1989, Caracas was to experience such a flashpoint where the government violently suppressed an uprising.

BANG! CARACAZO!

CHAPTER 4

EL CARACAZO

*Francie and I—Francie's 14-year-old son disappeared
during the Caracazo
Caracas, February 27, 2010*

"*The truth is that [El Caracazo] was a horror. People protesting
in the street against neoliberalism, against the shock programs
of the International Monetary Fund, against the privatization of
everything, against unemployment, hunger. And [the
government] sent us [army officers] to spray them with bullets
in the chest. And the political leaders, the supposed
democrats, talking about justice and democracy. That was no
democracy. It was a dictatorship of the [two primary] parties
and the elite, using the armed forces and using the media to
brainwash and confuse people. Here there was never
democracy.*"

Caracas

CARACAS, THE CAPITAL OF VENEZUELA, is a sprawling city of about six million in the greater metropolitan area. Being part of the Caracas Valley, some parts of the city scale steep hills and is separated from the Caribbean Sea by steep mountains.

The climate is usually temperate, but when I was there in 2009, it was very hot and there were rolling power brown outs due to a prolonged drought.

In May of 2011, the drought broke and flooding killed a couple of dozen people and displaced about six thousand—Chávez famously opened Miraflóres, his presidential palace, to some refugees from the flooding. The one thing that never surprises me, but still hurts, is to see homeless people living on the sidewalks within blocks from the White House in Washington, DC.

I have been to Caracas three times now and it is a crowded, dirty, and vibrant city. It is one of my favorite cities in the world, next to Havana. I guess I just like the Latin American Revolutionary flavor. I can't even compare Caracas to any other city of the world, except maybe for the sprawling confusion of Mexico City.

One of the most significant events in recent Venezuelan history occurred in Caracas beginning on a February morning in 1989.

27 Febrero, 1989

The uprising in Venezuela began on a quiet Monday morning in the Guarenas suburb of Caracas, when the residents went to the bus stops for the journey to downtown Caracas for their jobs—they found that due to CAP's deal with the IMF Devil, the fuel subsidies had been discontinued and transportation prices had risen 100% literally over night.

The poorer citizens of Caracas rely on buses to get to work, and the strict austerity measures that CAP referred to as "pacquete" (the "package") profoundly affected Caraqueños (being from or of Caracas) whose personal financial situations were already extremely precarious.

At the time of 27 Febrero, 1989, poverty in Venezuela was 70% and extreme poverty was at an unbelievable rate of 40%. As in today's USA, the income gap was widening and the "pacquete" was only going to make it worse.

By the end of that day, the uprising had spread to many places, Caracas included—transportation had been brought to a standstill, and even poor Venezuelans poured out of the hills to loot supermarkets and bodegas for staples like food and clothing. There were few, if any, reports of anything but necessities being taken.

On 28 Febrero, CAP, The Promise Breaker, suspended many constitutional guarantees and imposed a curfew. Then, tragically, CAP turned the nation's security apparatus, such as police and soldiers, against his own people and it's been estimated that between 500 and 3,000 people were killed and many of them were thrown into mass graves without their loved ones being able to retrieve the bodies for a proper burial.

I was in Caracas for the 21st commemoration of the Caracazo—literally, The Caracas Big One—or Caracas Explodes—and I was invited to attend a memorial for the victims and sit up on the stage with President Chávez as he gave a speech in an open plaza, surrounded by high-rise apartments, which made us all a little nervous. I asked my friend and hostess for the trip, Venezuelan-American attorney and author, Eva Golinger, where Chávez (a Venezuelan Army officer) was during the Caracazo and if he had been ordered to shoot his fellow countrymen and women.

Chávez was in bed with chicken pox at the time, but the violence horrified him and this spurred him to re-energize the

MBR-200 (Moviemento Bolivariano Revolutionario), the secret revolutionary society in the Venezuelan military that Chávez founded as a young instructor at a military academy, to begin planning for a coup against Carlos Andres Perez—which we will talk more about later.

I met Francie at the Caracazo memorial and we talked about our sons through our interpreter, Eva—and she told me that even though her son had been missing and presumed dead for 21 years, that she never stops missing him and she was sorry that I also had a son killed by the global elitist jackals for their profit.

The entire memorial was moving and meaningful to me, because not only is that day mourned, but many Venezolanos realize that the sacrifices of the people killed during the Caracazo led to the Bolivarian Revolution and, in turn, better living conditions for the survivors of that day and future generations, assuring that they would be able to continue the Revolution and keep growing towards a fairer standard of living for everyone.

The day that I sat on the stage with survivors and Revolutionary leaders, former disgraced murdering president of Venezuela, Carlos Andres Perez (CAP), was living comfortably in exile in Miami, Florida with other members of the Venezuelan and Cuban plutocracy who have had to flee (and take millions of dollars with them) from the masses who were awakened by a revolutionary spirit that transcends fear in its true hope for a better future for all.

The mass graves that CAP's security forces dug to bury its victims are still being discovered and excavated, but the remains of most of the victims will probably never be identified, if found at all. CAP's story isn't finished for the purpose of this book, yet—but he died in exile in Florida in 2011, living with a former secretary, his lover.

As previously stated, the Caracazo in 1989 was a major, groundbreaking event in Venezuela, but the seeds were planted for Chávez's rise to power and in the next chapter, we will see how that was done in a mostly peaceful and popular way.

CHAPTER 5
CULTIVATING REVOLUTION

"Comrades: unfortunately, for the moment, the objectives that we had set for ourselves have not been achieved in the capital. That's to say that those of us here in Caracas have not been able to seize power. Where you are, you have performed well, but now is the time for a rethink; new possibilities will arise again, and the country will be able to move definitively towards a better future."

~ Hugo
Chávez
After failed coup attempt against
then Venezuelan president Carlos Andres Perez
1992

HUGO CHÁVEZ AND HIS CO-REVOLUTIONARIES in the MBR-200 obviously were appalled at what the Venezuelan military was ordered to do by then president of Venezuela, Carlos Andres Perez (CAP) against its own citizens during the Caracazo.

Remember that Chávez was inspired by former Latin American

revolutionaries and was convinced at the time that a military overthrow was the only way to change the government.

Like many of us North Americans today, Chávez believed that the system was designed to keep everyone, who doesn't come to the contest with barrels of money and a plethora of corporate support, from breaking into the system.

I discovered this fact during the 2008 election season when I ran for Congress against then US House Speaker, Nancy Pelosi, in San Francisco. I am still recovering financially, spiritually, and emotionally from that campaign, and I am not afraid to admit it for instructional purposes.

The fraudulent US elections racket is totally designed to support candidates with the most money and only if the candidate affiliates with one of the major parties—we have a chapter about elections where we will go in-depth with former Democrat and former Congresswoman, Cynthia McKinney—but I just wanted to give you a preview.

Anyway, on February 4, 1992, Chávez led an unsuccessful military coup attempt against CAP. Although Chávez led five Army units into Caracas—as was his revolutionary assignment—he and his forces were betrayed and failed due to internal problems and these betrayals. He and some of the revolutionaries were holed up and cut off from the other units in other parts of the country, and their plan to take over the media, to broadcast the fact that the country was now under the rule of a revolutionary government, also failed.

Chávez was captured and allowed to go on Venezuelan TV before he was jailed for his part in leading the uprising. He famously told the people of the country that he loved and hoped to make better by his sacrifice, that the revolution had failed "por ahora," which means "for now." The attempt and the slogan electrified Venezuela that new and better ways were possible!

During the incarceration of Chávez he continued to read and correspond with members of the MBR-200 that weren't captured in February and a second attempt was made in November to oust CAP, which also failed.

However, the attempts greatly weakened CAP and he was impeached and removed from office in May 1993, not on the charges that he was responsible for ordering the murders of thousands of Caraquenos, but for the charges of misappropriating 250 million Venezuelan dollars.

Rafael Caldera who capitalized on the scandals of the CAP regime to gain the office of president in 1993, pardoned Chávez and his co-conspirators, freeing Hugo up to do something that he thought was impossible even the year before: win political power for the people by becoming the president of Venezuela in 1998.

During his campaign, Chávez promised the people that one of the first things he would do as president would be to call a People's Constitutional Referendum for the people of Venezuela, using their representatives, to write a new Constitution and put it up to a vote by the people of the nation.

In 1999, the Constitution of the Bolivarian Republic of Venezuela was ratified with a vote of 77% in favor—a major, major accomplishment for Chávez and the people.

SOME NOTABLE ACCOMPLISHMENTS OF THE NEW CONSTITUTION

ADDED A "PEOPLE'S BRANCH"

ADDED AN "ELECTION'S BRANCH"

CITIZENS ARE ABLE TO RECALL THE PRESIDENT

HEALTH CARE IS ENSHRINED AS A HUMAN RIGHT

EDUCATION IS ENSHRINED AS A HUMAN RIGHT

GENDER INCLUSIVITY IN THE LANGUAGE

EQUAL RIGHTS FOR WOMEN UNDER THE LAW

ONLY THE PEOPLE CAN AMEND THE DOCUMENT

AGGRESSIVE INDIGENOUS RIGHTS

COMMITS THE POWER OF THE STATE TO PROTECT THE ENVIRONMENT

One thing that I find so touching about this process, and giving power to the people, is that in the subsidized food markets each bag of rice and beans (Latin staples—not just in Venezuela) has one article of the People's Constitution printed on it.

With 350 articles, the People's Constitution is one of the longest and most comprehensive in the world.

WE THE ELITE

Most everyone reading this knows that the US has a Constitution that was written and ratified by the elite of this fledgling nation in the 1780s and was considered a "liberal" document at the time—again, one that Simón Bolívar admired during his lifetime.

Our Constitution has been amended 26 times and the process is not easy. The first 10 amendments, called the Bill of Rights, were written at the time of the body of the Constitution so its adoption by every state would be assured.

To end the evil twin stains of slavery and the disenfranchisement of women, many of our forbearers were forced to sacrifice much and even be killed fighting for rights that were peacefully claimed by the people of Venezuela in a very democratic process.

As to the fact that the Bolivarian Constitution has "aggressive indigenous rights," perhaps the only article in our Constitution that had anything to do with our indigenous peoples was the so-called Supremacy Clause that makes treaties the "Supreme Law of the Land." It's important to note that the US broke every single treaty it ever made with the native tribes.

HOW OBAMA AMENDS US CONSTITUTION

In Obama's short time in office, the "Constitutional Scholar" has almost unilaterally and figuratively amended our Constitution, which has a process that consists primarily of the elite changing it.

We the people have no right to recall the president or other federal officials and absolutely no right to amend it, short of an all out revolution.

Here is a partial list of Obama's "amendments."

CONTINUING CIA DRONE STRIKES IN PAKISTAN WITHOUT A DECLARATION OF WAR BY CONGRESS

WAGING WAR AGAINST LIBYA WITHOUT CONGRESSIONAL APPROVAL

REFUSAL TO PROSECUTE THOSE IN THE BUSH ADMINISTRATION RESPONSIBLE FOR ILLEGAL WAR AND TORTURE

DECLARING THAT HE HAS THE POWER TO EXECUTE AMERICANS WITHOUT TRIALS OR OTHER DUE PROCESS

EXECUTING AT LEAST THREE AMERICANS WITHOUT A TRIAL

MANDATING THAT US CITIZENS BUY HEALTH INSURANCE FROM PRIVATE CORPORATIONS

RENEWAL OF THE USA PATRIOT ACT

EXECUTIVE ORDER TO RESUME MILITARY TRIBUNALS AT GUANTANAMO BAY, CUBA

CHAPTER 6

THE CARE AND FEEDING OF REVOLUTION

THE ABOVE PICTURE IS THE METRO CABLE in San Agustin, Venezuela—soaring above the barrio with a back drop of the apartments that were built for the people who were displaced by the construction (apartments that were offered at very low-interest loans to the residents).

Unlike here in the USA where mountaintop or hillside living is very expensive, in some parts of the world, the poorest of the poor live on the sides of steep hills and mountains because of the lack of infrastructure: roads, power, and water.

Remember, just a short decade ago, illiteracy was rampant among the 70% of the population that was in poverty in Venezuela—President Chávez rose to power and made education one of the People Powers and through his educational program and missions, the literacy level has risen sharply—not up to Cuba's standards, but the poor of Venezuela are playing catch up.

So, one of the most miraculous things I saw in Caracas during my last trip was the Metro Cable in the barrio of San Agustin. Then, even though I have a touch of acrophobia, I rode it from the street up to the tiptop of a steep mountain. What is so miraculous about the Metro Cable?

Well, San Agustin is built on the steep slope of a very tall hill or short mountain. After the installation of the Metro Cable, the lives of the people of San Agustin were improved immeasurably. Before the Metro Cable, the residents—young, old, sick, pregnant, disabled, whomever—would have to walk up and down a dangerous set of steep stairs in all kinds of weather, but only if they wanted to go anywhere. If the residents of San Agustin wanted or needed food, supplies, water, or to go to work or school, they would have to make the strenuous and steep trek. There is a way to drive one's car part way up, but few people in the neighborhood own cars.

Even though I was terrified of heights before, I got on one of the cable cars and rode to the top—feeling a little queasy all the way because it does get pretty high off the ground! When we got to the top, we got to speak to the community organizers who made the cable car happen and the workers who come from the community.

This project was envisioned by the citizens of San Agustin, and from the very first meeting to the very first ride, a scant three years passed. The federal government partnered with the people of San Agustin—and paid for the construction, of course—but the feds took their direction from the community, not the other way around.

It costs one dime to ride the cable cars and, like I said before, has dramatically and overwhelmingly raised not only the barrio's standard of living, but the quality of life. After we rode up the cars, I had the experience of walking all the way down in the residents' "devious" way of showing me how hard it was. Just walking *down* made my legs shake like jelly and really opened my eyes in just a small way to the sacrifices that the more vulnerable in our world are forced to make by the very people that the Bolivarian Revolution are trying to replace with true change and true equalization of power and resources.

I have rarely witnessed righteous pride in a community's accomplishments as I saw in the formerly illiterate community organizers in San Agustin—our reward for walking down the treacherous hill was a delicious lunch served from the community soup kitchen that helps the residents of San Agustin supplement their monthly food stipend and what they can purchase with their wages. The group that hosted us in San Agustin consisted of mostly women who run the Neighborhood Council and were militantly pro-Chávez and pro-Revolution because he had fundamentally transformed their lives in profound ways. I was even shown one woman's new teeth that she received for free from Mission al Dentro (Venezuela's dental program).

The only thing I had to show *mi hermana* in Caracas was the permanent crown I have in my mouth that I am still paying for (and will be for years). It's pitiful that in our "wealthy" country, many of us have to go into lifelong debt or be bankrupted when health problems inevitably come our way. I am so happy that the "vulnerable" of Venezuela have a safety net and my sister can smile proudly without having to cover her mouth, ashamed of her rotten teeth.

With all of the successes, the Bolivarian Revolution has not been free from weeds or pestilent infestations, which we will touch on in the next chapter.

I think this is a good place to reprint the entire interview that I did with President Chávez, where, at the end, President Morales of Bolivia joins us. If you would like to hear the entire interview, please go to www.CindySheehansSoapbox.com and go to the archives and scroll down to March 14, 2010—the entire interview is there.

I was lucky enough to be able to fly down to Montevideo, Uruguay with President Chávez and his entourage who were traveling to attend the inauguration of Uruguayan president, Felipe "Pepe" Mujica. I finally caught up with President Chávez in his hotel in Montevideo.

Transcript of Cindy Sheehan's Soapbox Interview with President Hugo Chávez

Transcribed by Regina Freitag

Original Translation by Eva Golinger

Interviewer: Cindy Sheehan

Cindy Sheehan: Welcome to this video and audio audition of Cindy Sheehan's Soap Box.

Presidente Chávez, thank you for being on the show, thank you for this interview, and thank you for allowing me to bring the truth about Venezuela and about you and about your revolution to the people of the United States.

Before the revolution, Venezuela was a nation that was ruled and used up by the oligarchy, the elite. How did your revolution begin, how did it manage to remain relatively peaceful?

Hugo Chávez: Thank you Cindy, for this interview, for your efforts, that are so honorable and notable, to try to find out our truth and to contribute with its diffusion. And we wish you much luck in your struggles, which are ours as well, against war, for peace, for freedom and equality, and against imperialism. We accompany you in your struggles—you and the people of the United States. We love them the same. The bourgeoisie of Venezuela has always dominated the country, for more than a hundred years. And they dominated it with force, using violence, persecution, assassination, and disappearances.

Unfortunately, the Venezuelan history is a history full of a lot of violence, violence from the strong against the weak. In the 20th century, Venezuela, which was dominated by the oligarchy and the bourgeois state, the rich, the wealthy, produced a reversed type of miracle, we could say. Venezuela was the first exporter of oil from the beginning of the 1920s until the 1970s—one of the largest producers of petroleum in the world throughout all the 20th century. And when the 20th century ended, with the domination of the bourgeoisie, despite all the wealth, Venezuela had more than 70% poverty and 40% extreme poverty, misery, misery, misery.

So that generated an explosion, a violent one. All explosions are violent—an explosion of the poor, to liberate themselves. We were remembering just two days ago the Caracazo. You were there with us, with our people. Twenty-one years ago, the people woke, arose in a big explosion. And us military, we were used by the bourgeoisie to massacre the people, children, women, and older people. And then that awoke something in the young military folks, a consciousness of pain, and then we joined with the people. We had two rebellions, military rebellions, popular and (inaudible). A revolution isn't exactly peaceful. As you said it was relatively peaceful.

Cindy Sheehan: Yes, relatively, yeah

Hugo Chávez: Just like all true revolutions.

Cindy Sheehan: But doesn't the violence of revolutions sometimes come from the counter-revolution? And the Bolivarian revolution that has transferred power and wealth to the people is an inspiration and has remained relatively peaceful.

Hugo Chávez: Yes, we got to power in a peaceful way.

Cindy Sheehan: Right.

Hugo Chávez: Exactly, and we have been able to maintain it relatively peaceful. We've never used violence. They've used it against us. The counter-revolution. So the central strategy of our peaceful and socialist revolution is to transfer the power to the people. I'm sure you have been able to see some of it with your own eyes, in the neighborhoods of Caracas.

Cindy Sheehan: Yes I have.

Hugo Chávez: We have made immense efforts to help the people to be sovereign. When we talk about power, what are we talking about, Cindy? The first power that we all have is knowledge. So we've made efforts first in education, against illiteracy, for the development of thinking, studying, analysis. In a way, that has never happened before. Today, Venezuela is a giant school—it's all a school. From children of one year old until old age, all of us are studying and learning.

And then political power, the capacity to make decisions, the community councils, communes, the people's power, and the popular assemblies.

And then there is the economic power. Transferring economic power to the people, the wealth of the people distributed throughout the nation. I believe that is the principal force that precisely guarantees that the Bolivarian revolution continues to be peaceful.

Cindy Sheehan: Wonderful. In a speech the other day, you said that the United States demonizes you, demonizes Venezuela and the revolution. I of course have seen it with my own eyes and have been a defender of you and Venezuela and the revolution. Why do you think the Empire makes such a concerted effort to demonize you?

Hugo Chávez: I think for different reasons. But I've gotten to the conclusion there is one particular strong reason, a big reason. They are afraid, the Empire is afraid.

The Empire is afraid that the people of the United States might find out about the truth, they are afraid that something like that could erupt in their own territory—A Bolivarian movement; or a Lincoln movement—a movement of citizens, conscious citizens to transform the system. Imperial fear killed Martin Luther King. The only way to stop him was to kill him and repressing the people of the United States.

So, why do they demonize us? They know—those who direct the Empire—they know the truth. But they fear the truth. They fear the contagious effect. They fear a revolution in the United States. They fear an awakening of the people in the United States. And so that's why they do everything they can. And they achieve it, relatively, that a lot of sectors in the United States see us as devils. No one wants to copy the devil.

Cindy Sheehan: Right.

Hugo Chávez: Unless they are devils too. And the people aren't devils. The people are the voice of God.

Cindy Sheehan: Well, one of the biggest names they call you in the United States is dictator. Can you explain to my listeners and the people, for the benefit of this documentary, why you are not a dictator?

Hugo Chávez: In the first place, personally, I am against dictatorships. I'm an anti-dictator. We are here in Uruguay, in Montevideo. You know how many dictatorships were in this country—the Guerilla zone? I'm an anti-Guerilla. In addition to that, from a political point of view, I've been elected one, two, three, four times, by popular vote.

In Venezuela, we have elections all the time. Every year, we have elections in Venezuela. One time, Lula said, the president of Brazil... when he was in Europe, someone asked him: "Why are you friends with that dictator Chávez?" And Lula said a big truth: "In Venezuela, there is an excess of democracy. Every year there are elections. And if there aren't any, Chávez invents them."

Referendums, popular consultations, elections for governors, mayors; right now, soon we are starting national assembly elections, this year. In 2012 there is going to be a presidential election again. What dictator is elected so many times? What dictator convenes referendums? I'm an anti-dictator. I am a revolutionary—a democratic revolutionary.

Cindy Sheehan: Well, I have witnessed this revolution. I've witnessed the empowerment of the people of Venezuela, which is very inspiring, because the people in the United States don't feel this empowerment. I even rode the Metro Cable, and I'm afraid of heights. But I went out to San Agustin and then walked down the steps and saw how the so-called dictatorship has made the life of the people much better here in Venezuela. Also in the commemoration of the Caracazo you announced that you were again going to run for president in 2012. You've come a long way, but there is still a long way to go. What do you still think needs to be accomplished as far as infrastructure and the needs of the people in Venezuela?

Hugo Chávez: To tell you in a mathematical way, despite everything we've done in education, healthcare, infrastructure, housing, employment, social security, etc. But mathematically, I believe, of everything we've done and we have to achieve for the people, we have achieved about 10%. It's been 200 years of abandonment. The people have been abandoned. All the wealth of the country was in the hands of the elite. I talk about the bicentennial cycle—2010 to 2030—we have to work really hard in every aspect, infrastructure etc. I hope that you, in a few years, won't just go up in the Metro Cable in San Agustin, but all of Caracas is going to have metro cables, and everywhere, every place, housing, reconstruction in poor neighborhoods, the construction of new cities for the people and dignified housing, there is still a lot to do, to achieve what Simón Bolivar said. Bolivar taught us...

(President Evo Morales of Bolivia enters the room)

Hugo Chávez: Oh look! Evo is here. Evo, come and sit down! Bolivar taught us that the best government is the one that gives the people the best amount of happiness. That's our goal: the best, the largest amount of happiness.

My friend Evo, the president of Bolivia, who just got here, he is an indigenous leader! Brother how are you?

Evo Morales: Good, good.

Cindy Sheehan: Presidente Morales. Mucho gusto—so nice to meet you.

Hugo Chávez (introduces Cindy): Cindy Sheehan. She is a fighter for peace, against the war. She is a US citizen. One of her sons died in Iraq. So, she's interviewing us. And maybe you want to answer a question.

Evo Morales: (gives Indian blessing)

Hugo Chávez: To live well. It's a Mala Indian philosophy —To live well, the good life. To live well spiritually, intellectually, physically, that's what it's about.

Cindy Sheehan: Thank you, that's what it should be about. I have one final question.

Thank you for your generosity. This has been really wonderful. Maybe Presidente Morales could have some input about this too.

We see your rise to power in Venezuela as kind of a grassroots movement that has been spreading and has helped President Morales in Bolivia, and we see people all over South America taking back their power—because the power belongs in the hands of the people. A couple of weeks ago in the United States, a man flew his airplane into the tax building in Austin, Texas. Did you hear about that?

Evo Morales/ Hugo Chávez: Yes.

Cindy Sheehan: There is much frustration with the system. And there is a lot of that frustration in the United States. But instead of flying planes into buildings, we should find each other and organize. So, in the United States of course, we are now a system that is also for the elite, ruled by the elite, as a "Corporatocracy;" it's for the corporate elite. Of course, in my opinion, I believe the United States needs the same grassroots revolution, power back to the people that you've all had here in South America.

Can you leave us with some words of inspiration to encourage us, to give us the courage and heart for a true revolutionary change?

Hugo Chávez: We were the same, dominated, persecuted, and also there was a lot of desperation, just like that man who flew the plane into the building. There is a lot of that, a lot of the impulses, suicidal tendencies. Now, that's NOT the path. The path is consciousness, a conscious awakening. Evo was persecuted, from very young, I met him when he was an Assembly member, and they threw him out of Congress, and they persecuted him, they jailed him, a lot of his fellow strugglers died. And us too, we had our own experiences. A lot of our brothers died as well, a lot of us went to prison. But consciousness—that's why you're doing the right thing. The path is not to fly a plane into a building. It's to create consciousness—and then the rest will come on its own.

I'd like to take this moment to say hello to the people of the United States. And us here in the South, we have a lot of faith. And the people in the North are going to wake up. Just like you have awoken. Just like many have had awakenings. You can do great changes in the United States, and in a peaceful way, I hope. Because, what happens in the United States, those changes in the United States depend a lot...the future of the world depends on that a lot.

(Pres. Chávez addresses Pres. Morales) Evo, would you like to say something?

Cindy Sheehan: Please!

Evo Morales: I just finished a meeting with Eduardo Galliano.

Cindy Sheehan: Oh, I know him.

Evo Morales: He's so inspirational with the people, nature. Galliano is also going to the inauguration of Pepe Mujica. (Pres. Morales and Pres. Chávez talk to each other.) And he's going to bring some strategies, proposals, and we're going to have a meeting with Galliano and the cocoa workers...

Cindy Sheehan: Oh, very wonderful.

Evo Morales: To talk about equality and our experiences—the difficult things, how to unite us and to raise our consciousness for what you're talking about. The power resides with the people. I was just with Commandante Borhez, Thomas Borhez from Nicaragua. We were talking about issues of consciousness in Peru, in Colombia, on how to build a big political movement. But the issue is unity. In my experience, first the hated, the marginalized, we united first, the farmers and the indigenous. And from that it went on. Just like that unity, we need to do that with the political parties on the left and then the workers unite. Those are the forces that we have, that's the power that the people have—to get there is hard, you have to raise consciousness.

Cindy Sheehan: My documentary is called "We are all Americans." (Note—Subsequently changed) It comes from when I was being interviewed on Fox News and Sean Hannity told me how could I meet with the anti-American dictator Hugo Chávez. And I said: "But Sean, he is an American." We are all Americans and that's where the consciousness has to be raised and the unity has to come from in realizing that.

And so, it's been my highest honor to sit with you, Presidente, thank you for your hospitality and that of Venezuela and to finally meet you. I was invited to Bolivia to help to support you for your recall, but I was running for Congress against Nancy Pelosi in the United States. It was a bad time. I lost. (Laughs) I didn't win.

Hugo Chávez: But we will prevail.

Cindy Sheehan: We will be victorious. Thank you so much.

Hugo Chávez: We have to end, but I want to say something to you. Just about five days ago, we were in Cancun. We were on our way out from a hotel and the press was there, and there were some tourists—from California. So I went up to them and I said hi to a woman and her child and another woman—a lot of affection. It was spontaneous. And then I told my friends. I found tourists. I found US tourists: Older adults, young women, men, and adolescents. I've met with them in Japan, Moscow, and Beijing, in the Caribbean, everywhere in the world, in Buenos Aires. I've never felt one look of hate, but rather affection, so I think that despite everything, I believe the people of the United States in the depths of their hearts, they know how to appreciate where lies are and where the truth is. That's why we have such hope. And here is my heart for those people of the United States.

They call us anti-US-leaders, anti-American leaders, but we are not. We are anti-imperialist. But we love the people of the United States. We love humanity.

Cindy Sheehan: Muchas Gracias!

CHAPTER 7

WEEDS IN THE GARDEN OF REVOLUTION

"The dandelion is an excellent barometer, one of the commonest and most reliable. It is when the blooms have seeded and are in the fluffy, feathery condition that its weather prophet facilities come to the fore. In fine weather the ball extends to the full, but when rain approaches, it shuts like an umbrella. If the weather is inclined to be showery it keeps shut all the time, only opening when the danger from the wet is past."
Source: "Camping For Boys," by H.W. Gibson

Unfortunately, even though President Chávez has survived many attempts to undermine, demonize, and even overthrow his presidency and to quash the revolution, the "danger from the we(s)t" has certainly not passed!

Pertaining to ongoing current events, the NATO-UN-US assault on Libya and recent execution of Col. Gaddafi is a perfect example of what can potentially happen to Chávez.

The demonization of Chávez has not worked effectively (because the people of Venezuela are not stupid) yet, the undermining of the sovereign state is ongoing with the existence of the National Endowment for Democracy in Caracas; and even a blatant CIA coup attempt against him in 2002 failed—so what's next? A claim by the global plutocracy that Chávez is "killing his own people" without a shred of evidence could very well be on it's way, because just like Gaddafi of Libya, Chávez is the leader of a country that is wealthy with that black gold. Also similar to Gaddafi, Chávez has used the oil wealth of his nation to improve the lot in life of the poor in Venezuela.

In November of 2011, I flew to Cuba via Cancun, Mexico. On the way there, one of the many legs of the flight from Sacramento, California was from Salt Lake City to Mexico City.

I discovered that my row mates were from Venezuela, so I opened my photos on my computer and showed them a picture of Chávez and I together. Using my limited skills in Spanish, I finally got it through their heads that it was not "Lady Di" in the picture with Chávez, but me.

They said, "nosotros no te gusta, Chávez." (We don't like Chávez). And through their limited English and my limited Spanish, I figured out that they thought that Chávez has been very "good for the poor," but not so good for the rest of them. Judging from the fact that my friends had just flown all the way from Caracas to Salt Lake City to go shopping and had some very fancy duds, I figured that they probably weren't "the poor." It does illustrate, however, that the accomplishments of the Revolution and Chávez are noted and really, if not with admiration, with grudging acceptance.

Enough about my opinions, let's go directly to an expert in these matters, Venezuelan-American attorney and author, Eva Golinger. Eva has won many awards for her journalism and has been called "*La Novia de Venezuela*," (Venezuela's Sweetheart) by President Hugo Chávez himself. Eva has dedicated her life to the Bolivarian cause and she very diligently researched this topic and was able to get her findings into the hands of the President himself especially pertaining to the role of the

National Endowment for Democracy (NED), USAID, and the CIA in the coup attempt against Chávez.

Before we get to Eva, let's talk a little bit about the NED.

National Endowment for Democracy? Hmm...what a nice sounding name, isn't it? Really, who would be, who could be, should we be concerned about an entity that sounds so benevolent? Who doesn't love endowments and democracy?

This, according to the webpage of the National Endowment for Democracy:

The National Endowment for Democracy (NED) is a private, nonprofit foundation dedicated to the growth and strengthening of democratic institutions around the world. Each year, with funding from the US Congress, NED supports more than 1,000 projects of non-governmental groups abroad who [sic] are working for democratic goals in more than 90 countries.

After the Iran-Contra scandal of the '80s, then US president, Reagan, instituted the National Endowment for Democracy as a "kinder-gentler" version of the CIA (even though the CIA still operates globally with near impunity)—and indeed, it seems the NED is just a CIA front organization dedicated to the proposition of controlling foreign governments and inhibiting democracy in places like Venezuela where there is active energy to enfranchise and empower every citizen.

Even the Koch brother-financed, rightwing *stink-tank*, the CATO Institute, has denounced the NED.

In a paper by one of its analysts, Barbara Conry, entitled: *Loose Cannon: The National Endowment for Democracy,* (Nov. 8, 1993) she states:

The National Endowment for Democracy is a foreign policy loose cannon. Promoting democracy is a nebulous objective that can be manipulated to justify any whim of the special-interest groups—the Republican and Democratic parties, organized labor, and the US Chamber of Commerce—that control most of NED's funds. As those groups execute their own foreign policies, they often work against American interests and meddle needlessly in the affairs of other countries, undermining the democratic movements NED was designed to assist. Moreover, the end of the Cold War has nullified any usefulness that such an organization might ever have had. There is no longer a rival superpower mounting an effective ideological challenge, and democracy is progressing well on its own.

NED, which also has a history of corruption and financial mismanagement, is superfluous at best and often destructive. Through the endowment, the American taxpayer has paid for special-interest groups to harass the duly elected governments of friendly countries, interfere in foreign elections, and foster the corruption of democratic movements.

Our friend, Eva Golinger, has conducted extensive research into the crimes of the NED and USAID in Venezuela and, indeed, the organizations have spent millions of dollars since 1998 trying to defeat Hugo Chávez and the Bolivarian Revolution.

Eva is an undisputed expert on the false demonization campaign against Chávez. She talks eloquently of the reasons for that demonization campaign, her research into USAID and DAI (Developmental Alternatives, Inc.), and the "privatization of democracy promotion."

Let's hear from Eva now from a 2011 interview I did with her on *Cindy Sheehan's Soapbox*.

Eva Golinger: Precisely they (Americans) have that misconception because of how mass media has distorted and manipulated and generally lied about what has really happened here in Venezuela, and of course most of that is due to interest, corporate interest, as well as commercial interest, government interest, coming out of the United States in the case of Venezuela. Just a really brief history, which is important to understand why the mass media and even the US government would be taking such a hostile, aggressive position against the government of Hugo Chávez.

Venezuela is a very wealthy country in oil and gas reserves, it is actually one of the largest oil producers in the world, it has over 24% of oil reserves in the entire world, which is a lot for a country of 27 million people, and of course it's right close to the United States—I mean we're in the same hemisphere, it's the port of south America, it's only 2.5 hours approximately to fly to Miami and, in fact, Venezuela's maritime territory borders US territory, borders the colony of Puerto Rico, and so this is a very strategic place, and traditionally there have been governments before Hugo Chávez who were subservient to US interests. In fact, over the years, forty years after the fall of the last dictatorship in 1958, pretty much the governments here in place have been clients of the United States, it was a client state, and by the time Chávez got into power in 1998.

Venezuela had pretty much privatized most of the industries that had been public industries including communications, electricity, basic social services, health care, and the oil industry was on its way to being privatized, and of course to be privatized and handed over to US corporations.

When Chávez comes to power he changes all of that and he actually wins with a huge majority in 1998, coming out of a two-party system that his candidacy broke with—so very similar to the US in that sense—that there (was) a two-party system with a stronghold on power here, so Chávez breaks with that, and the majority of Venezuelans voted for him, precisely because they were tired and sick of the old corrupt system which had created poverty and basically destroyed the country and its infrastructure.

So this all begins to change when he gets power, and of course that effects different interests, and new laws were implemented, regarding land reform, regarding the redistribution of the oil wealth, and the whole hydrocarbon industry...this begins to effect really powerful interests, not just in Venezuela but outside Venezuela.

And then the years progress and Chávez himself gains more popularity, outside of Venezuela, and takes on a discourse that's much more anti-imperialist and nationalist at the same time, but also more socialistic, more humanistic. This begins again to sort of resuscitate all these old demons that the US government and the people of the US still hold very tightly regarding concepts of socialism and communism, particularly in this hemisphere.

And, you know, after all the prior decades throughout the 20th century when the US fought bitterly the rise of communism in this hemisphere, and had blockaded, inhumanely, Cuba for over 50 years and tried to isolate them and prevent and install dictatorships throughout the rest of the region in the '60s '70s and '80s in order to prevent the spread of Communism.

Now, here we have a government in the 21st century with all this oil wealth, this tremendous popularity, talking again about implementing a system that prioritizes social needs, and *redistributing the wealth, and all these things, and at the same time maintaining oil production, and then branching out with its relations, not just to the United States, but to other countries in the world, like China, like Russia, Iran, that in the end are helping to change the balance of power and lessen the influence and control of the US empire over the world.*

All of this obviously affects tremendously these powerful interests inside the United States, particularly, but all around the world, and have used their media power to try to demonize the image of President Chávez. It's much easier to try to remove a president from power or encourage regime change in a country if you can say that that head of state that you want to overthrow is a terrible person, is a demon, is doing awful things, is a dictator, so that's part of what this campaign against the person of Hugo Chávez in the international media has really been about. I mean in the end, here I've been living in Caracas for over five years, and I can tell you that this is the furthest thing from any kind of dictatorship. It's also not a communist state whatsoever, and in fact we're on the path to implementing a new sort of social model that we're calling socialism of the 21st century, but it's really a combination of capitalism and socialism and trying to figure out what works best and fits here in Venezuela.

Well, initially of course, as all throughout the world there was some Obama mania down here as well, throughout Latin America, and there was a lot of caution in the beginning of 2009 when Obama came to power and was elected, and was sworn in and inaugurated to the presidency there. There was caution to continue the same type of discourse denouncing US empire as strongly as it had been done during the Bush years—more so because of how it would impact world opinion, because so many countries around the world and of course the mass media had fallen in love with Obama, so anyone who would criticize Obama would be camped with the extreme right wingers or people who presented some kind of threat, in fact, towards Obama himself. There was a lot of concern about that as well, that if from out of Venezuela the president comes out attacking Obama and something happens to him, they're going to blame it on us down here or something like that.

So, yes, initially there was caution. I think there even was, in my own perception being a US citizen living down here, I'm a little sensitive to it, there was definitely a—that hope certainly did exist here, to put it in simple terms. I mean, not amongst myself or many others that are well aware that there is no change in the US empire, but yeah there was, and a lot of it was more due to Obama's skin color, and I mean his discourse, his poetic discourse, in reaching out his hand, extending his hand. I mean there was hope there would be some kind of change, and I remember, in fact, at the time of his election I was one of the only voices down here in Venezuela who openly rejected and deconstructed the Obama mania and what his image actually represented, and it was really just a continuation of the US empire.

But as the year progressed, as 2009 progressed, certainly, with the coup in Honduras, on June 28th and the military agreement between the US and Colombia to install military bases right next door to Venezuela, all of that whole masquerade of Obama and his hope and change began to fall, and now it's completely gone. Now everyone knows, there's no more hoping and waiting, and hoping there's going to be some kind of change in the US. People see it for what it is.

There was a moment where people thought, "Yeah it could happen, it's happening here," (Venezuela) that's part of it, that unlike people in the US, people in Venezuela have lived through a change like maybe some people wanted or hoped would happen with Obama. We've gone through it here, it has *happened, so there was a vision that maybe it was possible. Those of us who come from the US know really how it works, know that that was probably not going to happen, and it hasn't.*

Well he (Obama) did make some statement at the Summit of the Americas in the spring of 2009, trying to improve relations with Latin American countries, but a lot of it was fluff. It was just the speeches that had been written for him by his speech writers, and they sound good and all of that in front of Hugo Chávez and other representatives, Evo Morales from Bolivia and others that haven't had the best relations with the US over the past several years.

At the same time, yes, the most obvious sort of examples of how relations have gotten worse with Latin America and how actually my opinion as someone who has been investigating and analyzing US aggression and US policies in Latin America over the last decade, my opinion is that Obama's administration is much more dangerous towards Latin America than Bush's was, because with Bush we didn't have military bases being built throughout this region right next to Venezuela, and there's been a rapid sort of escalation in the aggression towards particularly Venezuela, but also Cuba. Obama did talk about somehow changing US policy towards Cuba but he, what he's done is make it worse, he's made it much more aggressive and hostile towards Cuba and, in many ways, is using certain words to try to distract from the actions of what his administration is really doing.

Particularly, we have the case of the coup in Honduras against President Zelaya that was a total scheme that had been concocted by Washington and its allies, of course, and the right wing, and the economic elite in Honduras, and the multinationals. Yet they used what they called the smart power, you know, Hillary Clinton's and Obama's new sort of strategy as opposed to soft power and hard power.

I mean, they [Hillary Clinton and Obama—ed.], used different discourse condemning the coup, but then not pushing really for the reinstatement of President Zelaya. I mean all kinds of things, and really just buying time. The process went on for so long that the coup was eventually consolidated and the US in the end has stepped forward as really the only country that has recognized an illegal government in Honduras and is funding it and supporting it.

Now it's all come out, but in the first few months, a lot of people were very wary to blame the Obama administration for any role in that coup in Honduras, which is incredible, because there hasn't been one single coup d'état in Latin America in history which hasn't been somehow managed and ordered by Washington. Why would that change under Obama?

Developmental Alternatives, Inc. (DAI) is a major US contractor, mainly conducting activities relating to what I call subversion and counterinsurgency, what they call, "promoting democracy abroad," and they've been handling, in Venezuela, an office of the US Agency for International Development (USAID), since 2002.

USAID was set up after a coup here against President Chávez, and it's called the Office for Transition Initiative. It's an office, it's a whole operation dedicated to regime change here in Venezuela, through other mechanizations other than the failed coup d' tat. So I've been following and investigating their (USAID) activities here in VZ. They've been funding now approximately $50 million over the last several years the opposition to President Chávez here—their political parties, their campaigns, their candidates, you know, we're talking major US intervention. It's a different kind, it's less visible, and I call it sometimes the "Silent Intervention."

What I found interesting is on December 13, last December 13 [2010], the NY Times wrote an article about a US citizen contractor, a contractor from the US, who had been detained in Cuba, and as it turned out he was working for this company, this US government contractor, Developmental Alternatives, Inc....that in fact, Developmental Alternatives Inc. had began working in 2009 under a contract, also with USAID and other US government agencies, to promote regime change in Cuba. And so this person was caught red-handed in Cuba distributing high-level satellite equipment to Cuban counter-revolutionaries and others to engage in some sort of clandestine operation there and he was detained.

So those two, the Venezuela-Cuba connection was easy to make with this company, and it seems the person who's been detained in Cuba's name has not been released, but the information I've received from inside sources do confirm it's one of these individuals at a high level that has been in charge of the VZ operation as well.

[The news] came out that when the CIA killings occurred in Afghanistan on December 30, it came out that also 15 days before, five contractors of DAI had also been assassinated. Then, on the killings on December 30 (2010), there was talk of contractors in addition to CIA officers that had been killed in that attack. In fact, on _DAI's website_ they have a statement about the December 15 killings, which received no attention, no media attention, despite the fact that five US citizens were killed in Afghanistan working for a USAID contractor, that one would not assume would be on a CIA operation, yet nothing was said about it in the media.

My speculation has to do with the fact that one of their operatives (Alan P. Gross) is detained in Cuba, just days before the December 15 killings, and they didn't want to call attention any more to that contractor, precisely because it is a cover for some sort of subversive activity to undermine democratic governments in general that don't support the US agenda.

What's most interesting, Cindy, is that article I wrote on my blog, Post Cards from the Revolution, *which is* Chávezcode.com, *I got contacted just a couple days ago by the president of Developmental Alternatives Inc., who wanted to have a face-to-face meeting with me and discuss my article and, basically, since we're not having a face-to-face since I'm in Venezuela, he sent me several messages, and one of them basically trying to intimidate me and accuse me of endangering DAI personnel by writing that article on my blog. And personally I found that quite interesting that the president of one of the US's largest contractors, with multibillion dollar contracts around the world, would even bother to contact little old me about an article written on a blog. Its not the* NY Times, *its not the* Washington Post, *its not the* BBC—*it's a blog on the Internet, but apparently I've hit a nerve there and something is coming out about an entity that no one's really ever heard of.*

You've heard of Blackwater, but you don't know who Developmental Alternatives is, well maybe until now, as the word gets out more. This is what I call the privatization of democracy promotion, just like the privatization of the US military and intelligence community via Blackwater and others, DAI is an entity that does similar services, but in what they call democracy promotion, which is just another strategy to obtain US imperialist objectives.

President Chávez is now in another political struggle with more elections taking place in October 2012.

Polling as of November 2011 shows Chávez with almost 60% of the votes for re-election. Knowing this, the US has dedicated about $20 million to the opposition's efforts to defeat Chávez (according to *Venezuela Analysis*).

What the heck? The US is violently suppressing movements here in the US—our "democracy" is based on how many dollars a candidate has—not on their integrity or work.

In my opinion, the US needs to clean its own home and recognize the sovereignty of other nations.

Chapter 8

"The Gates of Hell"

"Ooh, ah! Chávez will not go!"

*"I will go to the gates of Hell, if I have to,
to defend the people of Venezuela."*

~ President Hugo Chávez before the April 11, 2002 coup

YES, THE US SPONSORED AND SUPPORTED a coup against a democratically elected president in South America on April 11, 2002. I know it's hard to believe that the US would do something so sneaky, underhanded, undemocratic, and reprehensible (snarkiness), but it has been well documented that the US was behind the coup—which transformed into a coup attempt two days later, when Chávez returned to power.

Recently, the world discovered that Chávez is battling something even scarier than the US Empire, and that's a battle with cancer. He has tried to assure the people in Venezuela, and we outside the country, that he will beat it like he has beaten the coup and many electoral challenges—including a recall sponsored by the US and the opposition in 2004. We also learned that a tumor was successfully and completely removed, but it is still a frightening diagnosis for Chávez, his family and his fledgling people's democracy. Remember, in the historical scheme of things, Venezuela has only been a people's democracy for about 12 years now—the US has been an elitist democracy for 235 years—and we seem to be going backwards in terms of participatory democracy.

This brings us to a peripheral subject around the 2002 coup against the Bolivarian Revolution: will the revolution survive without its dynamic leader, if something happens to Chávez? Because there was much rejoicing among the opposition in Venezuela (and indeed in the US) and seeming confusion among the rest when he was missing in Cuba for those days of his surgery and treatment, it seems like the predators are ready to pounce on any opportunity to derail the people's revolution.

The opposition in Venezuela, as I have pointed out, consists mostly of the deposed oligarchy and those who have a little tiny bit less because the poor there are gaining more, albeit too slowly for them. The opposition jumped on the confusion around the president's illness to call for his resignation and for the vice president to take over—against the Bolivarian Constitution that says the president may be absent for 180 days without losing his office.

The corporate media in Venezuela and around the world had already killed Chávez in apparent "wishful thinking" reporting. Indeed, freak of nature, Dick Morris (Clinton advisor turned Republican "strategist" and Faux News regular), tweeted that we should all, "Take a moment out from your day to pray for the death of Hugo Chávez." What a "god" that sick Dick must have that listens to prayers for the death of one of its children! And, a friend of mine up in Canada urgently messaged me one night saying that Canadian CNN had already confirmed the untimely death of Chávez. He's still alive and kicking, so I will write some brief words about the coup attempt.

There are millions of words written about the 2002 coup (and a great documentary called: *The Revolution Will Not Be Televised)* against the Bolivarian Revolution and its leader—so I will try and give you the Campbell's Soup (condensed) version.

We all know, now, that against all odds, Hugo Chávez won the presidential election in Venezuela by a landslide electoral victory in 1998 and ascended to power in 1999. Along with a referendum to re-write the Constitution to make it a people's document, he used very strong and inflammatory rhetoric against the country's Robber Class. He called them "esqualidos," or the "squalid ones." Wasteful and resentful is a perfect way to describe Earth's Robber Class, but not a good way to build bridges and coalitions. I, for one, like the inflammatory approach, because it gets people thinking and moves people to your side with cleverness and honesty. Chávez's rhetoric did have that affect on a lot of people, but not the ones that owned Venezuela's media.

Already, in 2002, there was a concerted effort to undermine the revolution. Ari Fleischer, the spokes-liar for the Empire at the time, seemed to be waging a one-man demonization campaign against Chávez.

Ari Fleischer, who worked for the confessed liars of the Bush administration, stood before the US public and told lie after lie about 9/11, Afghanistan, Iraq—why should we have believed, or believe today, anything that comes from any US administration, but the Bush crime family seemed to be particularly scandalous.

A typical comment about Chávez from Fleischer would go something like this: *"The regime of President Chávez has been controversial and not met with popular support."* The aforementioned National Endowment for Democracy, CIA, corporate media—and the Bush crime family manufactured controversy against Chávez. Does any government have 100% support of the people who live there? In our own country, the approval ratings of the government continue to spiral down while the wars abroad and, domestically, economic terrorism hits us harder by the day.

George Tenet, former director of the CIA under the Clinton and Bush crime families, and one of the most profoundly criminal jackasses that ever served in a position overpopulated with criminal jackasses, testified before Congress and, with a look of incredulity and a voice dripping with indignation, said that Chávez didn't appear to have "the interests of the United States at heart."

Excuse me? I suppose the CIA is quite accustomed to most world leaders placing the interests of the USA ahead of their own country, (or be murdered, deposed, or?) but why? If more leaders were like Chávez and had the guts to stand up to the US and say that the interests of their country are more important than the US, then, in my opinion, the world would be a more peaceful and prosperous place to live upon.

EVENTS LEADING TO COUP ATTEMPT

| 1998 | Hugo Chávez elected president of Venezuela in landslide. |
| 1999 | People Power rewrites the Venezuelan Constitution. |

October 2001　Chávez shows pictures of Afghan children murdered by the US invasion on Venezuelan TV and calls on the US to stop: "The massacre of the innocents. Terrorism cannot be fought with terrorism."

November 2001　　"Enabling Act" about to expire

*(An **enabling act** is a piece of legislation by which a legislative body grants an entity which depends on it for authorization or legitimacy the power to take certain actions. For example, enabling acts often establish government agencies to carry out specific government policies in a modern nation state. The effects of enabling acts from different times and places vary widely).*

49 new laws passed under the Enabling Act by new legislature comprised of mostly "Chávistas."

Among the most controversial:

Land Reform Act (Mission Zamora)

In the event that private land-owners fail to make their land productive, the law states that high-quality private land over 100 hectares (roughly 250 acres) or low-quality land over 5,000 hectares (12,355 acres) can be expropriated—with the government compensating the owners at market price.

Oil Law

Doubles royalties from oil companies to the government of Venezuela to be used to fund mostly social programs. Also, began to consolidate and nationalize more petroleum operations under PdVSA (Petroleós de Venezuela S.A.) state oil company. Oil was nationalized in Venezuela in 1978, but the profits were still beneficial to a few.

February 2002 Four military officials, including a general and a (dismissed) rear admiral, publicly call on Chávez to resign.

02.07.02 Venezuelan Air Force Colonel Pedro Vicente Soto and National Reserve Captain Pedro Flores Rivero lead a rally protesting the Chávez government's allegedly undemocratic and authoritarian practices. (Apparently, the Venezuelan Military were a little miffed that it had been asked to perform civil service)

04.04.04 Members of PdVSA (state oil company) begin a strike.

04.07.02	Chávez fires seven board members of PdVSA on his TV show, *Aló Presidenté*
04.09.02	Some trade unions and the national Chamber of Commerce (Fedecameras) call for a general strike to protest the firing of the PdVSA board.
04.11.02	Venezuelans gather to begin what many of them thought would be a rally and peaceful march, but the march gets diverted to the presidential palace, Miraflóres, by multi-millionaire businessman, Pedro Carmona (President of the Chamber of Commerce, Fedecameras), and the Confereración de Trabajadores de Venezuela, CTV.

The Mayor of Caracas, who was not a Chávista, calls the move "irresponsible" because supporters of Chávez were already gathered at Miraflóres and he rightfully feared a violent confrontation.

Twenty protesters (mostly pro-Chávez) were killed in the ensuing melee and 110 were wounded. Opposition TV and other media shows footage of Chávez supporters shooting at something—which the media said was peaceful demonstrators, but it turns out the footage was manipulated and false—they were actually defending themselves from anti-Chávez snipers. Later footage shows pro-Chávez demonstrators being shot upon from rooftops.

The opposition shuts down transmissions from state TV.

"Chávez supporters defending themselves"

04.12.02   Anti-Chávez forces surround the palace, demand his resignation, or threaten to bomb the palace. To avoid further bloodshed, Chávez agrees to be escorted away and is taken to La Orchila, yet he refused to resign.

Opposition leaders and opposition media spread the lie that Chávez resigned. The ministers and staff loyal to Chávez begin to call media to dispute the lie that Chávez resigned—that he was forced out.

Pedro Carmona of Fedecameras takes over as president of Venezuela and disbands the legislature and Supreme Court to loud cheers from the coup plotters, the nation's oligarchy.

"Pedro Carmona sworn in after coup"

04.13.02   US Ambassador to Venezuela, Shapiro, meets with Pedro Carmona for over an hour, and refers to him as "president."

Most Latin American nations condemn the coup.

Thousands of citizens loyal to Chávez and/or upset that their votes are in the process of being violently taken away from them in an illegal power grab, begin to gather at Miraflóres.

Palace guards plot to retake the building. The guards take up key positions and, at a prearranged signal, take members of the new government prisoner.

State television is restored and broadcasts calls for the military to back the return of Chávez.

Full control is returned to the Chávez administration and Chávez triumphantly returns.

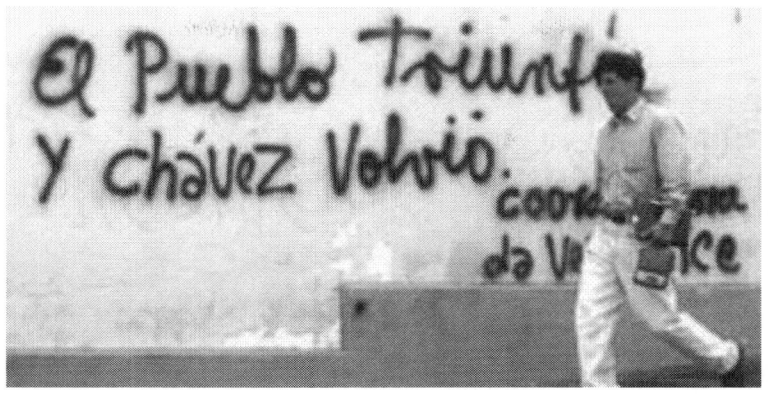

"Power to the people and Chávez returned"

Chapter 9:

Elections Fraud "R" US

"I might project results that will be much more satisfactory than they were in 2000 in Florida."

~ Former US President, Jimmy Carter,
Observing the 2004 recall effort against President Chávez

HUGO CHÁVEZ HAS BEEN PRESIDENT OF VENEZUELA since 1999—12 years now—here in the US, we are not used to such longevity in the office of president.

There were officially no term limits to that office in the US, but there was a custom, set by the first president, to only hold the office for two terms. That custom was disregarded by FDR and he died at the beginning of his 4th term. After his death, the 22nd Amendment to the Constitution was ratified that limited future presidents to two terms—but of course, the entitled Congress, whether in the House or Senate, has no such limits.

I must admit that, initially, I had some reservations about the number of years that Chávez has been in office. I used to be a vocal protagonist of term limits as electoral reform, but I am no longer one.

The argument against term limits is that they are undemocratic. What if an elected official is actually working for the people and the people want him or her in office? It's not like our system where more than 95% of incumbents are regularly sent back to Congress no matter what they do. Our system is also very undemocratic in the way that elections are manipulated with advanced hanky-panky, or the way the electorate is manipulated through advanced propaganda techniques.

Of course, the National Endowment for Democracy and its parent company, the CIA, have spent millions in Venezuela trying to overthrow Chávez, whether electorally or violently, and one of the first accusations hurled at him from propagandists here in the US, after he survived every re-election, recall, or referendum is, "fraud." My mother would have said, "That's like the pot calling the kettle black."

For this documentary, um book, I wanted to talk to the top experts in their fields and I scored interviews with some amazing people—for US election fraud and many other fascinating topics—my first pick was ex-Congresswoman, and my friend, the Honorable Cynthia McKinney.

What follows is my edited (for length) interview with Ms. McKinney.

I interviewed Cynthia in a warm studio in Atlanta, Georgia in the summer of 2009—but the interview below is still relevant and fascinating. Cynthia and I are very comfortable with each other and I hope her humanity can shine up from the page to your eyes and into your heart.

I supported Cynthia when she ran for president in 2008—and voting for her was the 2nd proudest vote I ever cast (voting for myself for Congress edged Cynthia out a wee bit), and every day that she is dodging bombs, or demonization campaigns, working for peace and justice, makes me even more proud of her and relieved that I voted for such a courageous, compassionate, and intelligent person—not the dog and pony show we currently have "running" this nation. Obama, like the one before him, plays fast and loose with facts, and the children of others.

The Interview

Sheehan: Cynthia, thank you so much for agreeing to be a part of our documentary (now, book).

McKinney: Cindy, you are my friend, you are my inspiration, and you are my leader.

Sheehan: Likewise. So, when we started getting into the charges of Venezuela electoral fraud, we wanted to talk to somebody about US electoral fraud and you were our first choice. We're really happy that you were available to do this.

One of the things that the ruling class of the world, not just the US, will say about President Chávez is that he is illegitimate because there is election fraud in Venezuela and that they fix the elections. We know that elections have been fixed since the beginning of time, no matter how hard you try to make them legitimate, there's always some way to mess around with them. But people like yourself, and Robert Kennedy, Jr., Bev Harris, Bob Fitrakis in Ohio, and Greg Palast, you've brought to light the overt electoral fraud here in the United States, especially in 2000 and 2004, and not only is there election fraud but there's just millions of instances I think of disfranchisement of people of color voting. Could you detail some of the abuses of not only electoral fraud in the United States but disenfranchisement?

McKinney: I think we really have to start with the founding fathers, who felt that the people who look like me were only 3/5 of a person to be counted.

Sheehan: I wasn't even in the Constitution.

McKinney: That's exactly right.

Sheehan: People that look like me weren't even in the Constitution

McKinney: So, we begin with an imperfect democracy, and we have to understand that, and the challenge of various movements in our country has been to perfect our union and so, of course, we have had women who fought for probably 75 or 80 years for the right to be able to cast a vote. And we have black people whose struggle for the right to vote is legendary, and most recently we have our more recent immigrants who have come to this country who are language minorities, and they too have had to struggle to be included in our representative government.

So, with an imperfect foundation, what are some of the manifestations we have seen recently that would give us pause as we say we are going out into the world to bring democracy to the rest of the world? Well, of course, we can't take democracy anywhere if we don't have it at home. You have to have it to share it. And we don't have it. Why do I say that?

Not only because of those people who were never included in the idea of enfranchisement, of the founding fathers, but the whole struggle to include people from every shape and language and color and hue and ethnicity so that they could have a place in our republic.

Now, in 2000 I guess you can say that was almost the pinnacle of disfranchisement, because you had a group of people to sit in a room and decide whose vote was going to be counted and whose vote was not going to be counted. Who was going to be allowed to vote and who was not going to be allowed to vote, and who was going to win the election, and who was going to be prevented from winning an election. All that came about in the 2000 election for president and there, on the backs, really of black people's hopes and aspirations and frustrations, where black people almost had a 100% turnout in Florida.

They (black voters) were angry, because Jeb Bush was the governor and he had designed a program to do away, to get rid of, affirmative action, so black people were angry and said "We're going to show George W. Bush," and so you had the kind of participation rates that you've never had. You had them in Florida. And it just so happened that it was in Florida that the massive disfranchisement of the black voter took place

Sheehan: How did that happen? How did they do that?

McKinney: Well, basically, somebody somewhere decided they would use the convicted felon's lack of voting rights to their advantage, to the Republican Party's advantage. We know that we've got social injustice, criminal injustice that's administered by the justice department in our country, so therefore blacks bare the brunt of this problem of convicted felons.

And because the majority of those people, who in certain states convicted felons cannot vote and, therefore, Florida happened to be one of those states. So what happened was the states where there were republican governors sent their lists of convicted felons to Florida, which had Jeb Bush, George W. Bush's brother, as its governor. So you had Christy Todd Whitman from New Jersey send down her list of convicted felons. You had George W. Bush who was the governor of Texas send over his list. You had the Ohio list come down to Florida. All these Republicans are sending over these names of convicted felons. But guess what? That was against the law, but they did it anyway—and got completely away with it.

Sheehan: I understand that even people with similar names got their name crossed off the Florida voting roles.

McKinney: That's right, so James Smith, who was a convicted felon in Ohio, became a convicted felon in Florida. So when James Smith in Florida, who is not the convicted felon in Ohio, decides that he wants to go and vote because he wants to show George W. Bush a thing or two, when he arrives at the voting place Mr. Smith is told, "You're a convicted felon, and you can't vote."

This is Election Day, there's nothing that Mr. Smith can do about it. Well, there should have been something that he could do, and that's what we saw in 2004. There's something called a provisional ballot, so then if Mr. Smith goes to the polling place and they tell him, "Well, you're a convicted felon," but Mr. Smith says, "I am not a convicted felon, I want to vote," then he's supposed to be given a provisional ballot on which to vote.

The only problem is the provisional ballot didn't count.

Sheehan: Was that in the Help America Vote Act?

McKinney: Yes, which is what funded the electronic voting machines, which is another layer in the way in which voters in the United States were disfranchised. Now it starts out that you're targeting the black vote for disfranchisement. Those people in 2000 were going to make sure they have machines that don't work, were going to make sure that they don't have enough machines, were going to make sure they had confusing looking ballots—anything that could confuse the voter—that was done in 2000, in fact, including dispatching police to the precincts so they would establish roadblocks and check points.

Now if you happen to have an outstanding warrant, or some reason that you would not want to pass by the police, then you can't go to vote, because that's where the police are. All of this was done in 2000. But it wasn't just done in Florida; it was done all over the country. But people paid attention to Florida because of the Electoral College, which is another way voters in the United States are disfranchised; it all came down to Florida and the electoral votes in Florida.

Sheehan: Tell us why the 2000 vote in Florida was so important to black people.

McKinney: I don't want to say black people were agitated; they were motivated, they were motivated for various reasons; first of all, you also had the upcoming, in 2001, Durbin World Conference Against Racism. So you had various organizations all over the United States that were connecting with each other.

You had the black community connecting with the Latinos and the Native Americans and the Asians and the progressive whites, we were all working together, building towards the 2001 Durbin World Conference, and then they were also able to feel empowered because they were working with the African continent, they were working with Europeans who were very supportive at a certain level—not at the governmental level but at a certain level, the grass roots level, they were very supportive.

People in Asia were supportive, and the indigenous people, they were supportive throughout Latin America. So there was this synergism and that was very, very real all over the United States. That was one thing.

Then, there was also the fervor that had been particularly directed toward the people in Florida, because George W. Bush's brother was the governor of Florida.

So you've got the governor of Texas, and his brother is the governor of Florida—now Texas is like number two or three most populace state in the country, and you've got Florida which is like number three or four most populace state in the country. So you've got one family controlling at least two of the top five states in the entire United States. Jeb Bush had done the race politics and was trying to erase affirmative action, and the black community was very motivated to show George W. Bush that not only are we going to show you a thing or two, but we're going to get rid of your brother come next election.

Sheehan: A lot of people, even so-called progressives, especially Democrats, want to blame Ralph Nader for Gore's loss in Florida. Can you dispel that myth?

McKinney: Well, you know, the Democrats have a vested interest in blaming someone else, because the voters that are most loyal to the democratic party are black voters, and it was black voters who were completely disfranchised in Florida, and it was on the black vote and the denial of the black vote that George Bush schemed his way along, with those around him in the Republican party, to the White House.

Then the Democratic Party had something to say about a stolen election. But guess what? They didn't say anything. You had the person who lost the election (who actually won the election), Gore. Gore told people, don't protest, and when Gore had the opportunity to say let's recount the entire state of Florida, and then they would have found the tens of thousands of black votes that were never even counted, Gore just said, "Let's pick this precinct and this precinct and this precinct," so it was a token effort.

The people, who were really left holding the bag, were the black voters who supported Al Gore. So, black voters were stabbed in the back by the Democratic Party.

Now the Democratic Party can't say: "We're sorry, we didn't do what we should have done." They can't say that, because they rely on the black vote exclusively.

You see, this is at a time of redistricting, when the Democratic Party in particular wants to have enough blacks in a district so they can win, but not enough blacks so they can have self-determination in that district. (This is the game that will be played out in the next few years as we go through the census and reapportionment and redistricting.) And the Democratic Party didn't do that. The Democratic Party allowed the theft by the failure to count black votes to stand.

So they (Democrats) look for someone else to blame. And of course, there's the third party candidacy of Ralph Nader, so they like to blame Ralph Nader. The fact of the matter is, if all of the votes in Florida alone had been counted, if they had just demanded that the black votes be counted, Al Gore would have won Florida, and he would have won the election. It's on the Democrats that they let down their most loyal voters, and they let down the country, and as a result of George W. Bush's policies: *the Democrats let the world down.*

END OF INTERVIEW (part two is in the appendix)

See?

In 2004, an anti-Chávez NGO called Sumaté sponsored a recall effort against Hugo Chávez in Venezuela. The USA's Jimmy Carter and the Carter Center went down there to observe, and perhaps certify, the election if it was valid. I will close this chapter with Carter's own words:

President Jimmy Carter: Venezuela Election Trip Report

August 13-18, 2004
By Jimmy Carter

August 19, 2004

After leaving Georgetown, I arrived in Caracas in the evening of 8/13 and was briefed by Ambassador Shapiro, Jennifer McCoy, Francisco Diez, Rachel Fowler, and other staff members of The Carter Center. I gave them an assessment of my visit to Guyana, and they reported high tensions in Venezuela with the approach of the referendum revocatorio scheduled for 8/15. The next morning I met with Organization of American States Secretary General Gaviria, with former presidents Raul Alfonsín and Eduardo Duhalde, both of Argentina, Belisario Betancur of Colombia, and Rodrigo Carazo of Costa Rica, and then our Carter Center staff to discuss our common approach to our monitoring duties.

Excluding the presidents, our group then met with President Chávez for about two hours. He appeared quite confident but pledged to resign immediately if he should lose the referendum vote and said in that case he would rest for a week and then resume campaigning for re-election. Toward the end of our meeting, I called on him to be gracious in victory, to make every effort to reunite the divided country, and to let us help in establishing a forum for dialogue between the government and opposition groups. He did not respond directly but was very quiet while I spoke and then said he had always wanted the nation to be united. Subsequently, he said he needed to spend more time with me and asked if we could have lunch together on Monday.

We then visited the National Electoral Council headquarters (CNE), where many of our questions were answered, including some about last minute personnel changes in the local polling places and election workers, and our access to all aspects of the voting procedures. In general, we were satisfied. We then met with military leaders, whose forces have always played a major role in elections. The minister of defense finally agreed to abide by all CNE directives and to cancel the military's plan to examine all voter ID cards, which may be seen as intimidation.

Our next meeting was with opposition leaders, where we heard a litany of catastrophic predictions about cheating, intimidation, and actual violence planned by the government for election day. We reported on the assurances we had received from CNE and the military, which answered most of their concerns.

Gaviria and I then had an overflow press conference, where we were able to answer many questions that had been raised about our freedom as observers and about rumored plans of the CNE and military. Our last meetings of the day were with state-owned and privately-owned news media. The latter group predicted that there would be violent attacks on their property and said that government military forces would not protect them. I promised to share their concern with the minister of defense, and he honored my request to strengthen security.

We were out early on election morning and were amazed at the incredibly large turnout, with thousands of people waiting in line an hour before polls were scheduled to open. Venezuela has a system of electronic voting (with a paper ballot backup) and voters' thumbprints are recorded electronically, transmitted by satellite, and compared almost instantaneously to prevent multiple voting. A "No" vote supported Chávez, and a "Yes" vote called for his removal from office. Starting was somewhat slow, but 99.5 percent of the voting machines were on the line by 10:30 a.m. Some of the fingerprint operators did not report for duty, but this was not permitted to interfere with voting. The great waiting crowds were in fine spirits, cheering loudly everywhere we showed up.

During the day, the opposition leaders presented to us and their supporters what turned out to be erroneous exit polling data that showed Chávez losing the vote by 20 points or more, and they also sent this information to their own people and to foreign news media. However, the news media honored the CNE ruling against broadcasting any kind of alleged voting results domestically. In the meantime, long voter lines remained intact past the 4 p.m. closing time, past an extended 8 p.m. closing time, and until midnight, when they finally closed. A few people voted as late as 3 a.m.

At about 12:30 a.m., we and OAS leaders were invited to witness the disclosure of the first electronic tabulation, which showed "No" votes at 57 percent and "Yes" votes at 43 percent among the 6.6 million votes counted at that time (of 10.5 million expected to vote). Gaviria and I decided to invite the private media owners and opposition leaders to my hotel suite to let them know about this and to tell them that this was compatible with our own quick count results. The media owners and some of the opposition said they would accept our judgment while others were angry. We urged them to check their own sample voting results and stated that we would obtain updated figures next morning before making a public declaration of our judgment. We were in Venezuela to remain neutral, to observe the electoral system, and to make a careful and sound final assessment regarding whether the will of the people is expressed. Chávez called me, and I urged him to wait on any claim of victory until after a CNE public announcement and to be generous and positive in his victory statement. He promised to do so.

Finally, after three hours, we offered to the still irate opposition leaders our services in resolving any of their remaining doubts before we had to leave (after two more days). Having insisted all during election day on a 20 point defeat for Chávez, their pollster (Súmate) admitted before leaving that their data now showed only a five point defeat and that quick count data were still being received. Early the next morning, they reported that these results were reversed, with 55 percent supporting Chávez, but opposition leaders still were claiming massive fraud and a victory for their side. Final voting results, including the centers with manual ballots, showed 59-41 in favor of Chávez, with his victory in 22 of the 24 states.

Gaviria and I had another press conference early in the afternoon on Monday to confirm the legitimacy of the CNE returns. I called Secretary of State Colin Powell to report our authentication of results, and he promised to issue a statement from Washington endorsing our findings.

On Monday, we had supper with Chávez and found him eager to begin substantive dialogues with responsible opposition leaders who are willing to reciprocate. We urged him to show generosity to Súmate and some others who are being accused of crimes going back to the coup against him and to ensure a balanced membership of CNE as local and state elections are planned late in September. He was receptive to these suggestions and supported an additional audit of electronic paper ballot backups from the machines that would assuage any remaining doubters.

Although the country was peaceful, some opposition leaders were still in anguish, as indicated by Tuesday morning newspaper editorial headlines, "Catástrofe," "El Fraude Permanente," and "Serias Dudas." After meeting with Súmate and other opposition representatives who claimed there were differences between paper ballot backups and electronically transmitted results, we agreed to have a second audit process to double check the correlation. We made it clear to them and to the public that this did not imply any doubt by The Carter Center or OAS regarding the integrity of the electoral process or the accuracy of the reported results.

After making these arrangements, we met with Catholic bishops and then had a final supper with a group of about 20 empresarios.

Jennifer McCoy and Rachel Fowler stayed in Caracas to oversee the second audit of the machines that we will do with the OAS and the CNE.

Chapter 10

Obama vs. Chávez

(Fake Hope vs. Revolution)

WHILE ON MY WAY TO INDIANA FOR SPEECHES around the 10th anniversary of the invasion of Afghanistan, Obama's "good war" is not going so well for anybody, and only 37% percent of those polled (I heard from a TV in the airport) feel that Obama will be re-elected in 2012.

Also, a CBS poll that I read today shows that over six out of every 10 Americans thinks the US should end the seemingly endless war in Afghanistan.

In 2011, there was an "Arab Spring," "European Summer," and it looks like with growing protests on Wall Street and elsewhere in the nation, we may have an "American Fall," after the first decade of the new century belonged to Latin America.

In September of 2011, Obama introduced a half billion dollar jobs' bill that will, of course, go nowhere in the House of Representatives, because in 2010, the Republicans regained majority in the House. This brings up a very interesting question: If Obama were so concerned about the high unemployment rate, as his teleprompter-robotic-grave tone indicates, then why didn't the Democratic White House and Democratic Congress pass a jobs' bill when the party had a super-majority for the first two years of Obama's presidency? Hmm...I tend to think that maybe the plutocracy really doesn't want to put Americans back to work—OR, desperate labor is cheap labor and the so-called 1% needs to end the practice of the working-class getting really uppity with our labor organizing and demands for a good wage, good benefits, and safe workplaces?

I am not interested in "re-inventing the wheel," and my dear friends at St. Pete's for Peace in St. Petersburg, FL, keep a comprehensive and current webpage on the "accomplishments of the Obama regime."

Here are a few lowlights:

- Waged war on Libya without Congressional approval
- Started a covert, drone war in Yemen
- Has ordered troops into Uganda
- Escalated a proxy war in Somalia
- Escalated the CIA drone war in Pakistan

- Maintained the military operations in Iraq
- Sharply escalated the war in Afghanistan
- Secretly deployed special forces in 75 countries
- Sold a record $60 billion of weapons to Saudi Arabia
- Signed an agreement for 7 military bases in Colombia
- Touted nuclear power as "safe," even after the disaster in Japan
- Opened up more area to deepwater oil drilling, even after the BP disaster in the Gulf of Mexico
- Recorded a TV commercial promoting "Clean coal"
- Defended body scans and pat-downs at airports
- Signed the USA PATRIOT ACT extension into law
- Continued Bush's illegal rendition program
- Has kept Guantanamo prison camp open
- Extra-judicially executed at least 3 US citizens in Yemen— one a teenage boy with at least 12 of his companions
- Vowed to seek "toughest sanctions" against Iran for the extremely alleged Iranian plot to assassinate the Saudi Arabian ambassador in the US
- Waved penalties on countries that use child soldiers
- Refuses to show proof of killing Osama bin Laden invading the sovereign nation of Pakistan to allegedly do so
- Reauthorized embargo against Cuba
- Quietly approved sale of illegal bunker buster bombs to Israel
- (Not so) secret drone bases constructed in Africa and Arabian peninsula
- Read a more extensive exposition of Obama's "change" at St. Pete's for Peace

I really want to thank my friends at St. Pete's for Peace for having the integrity to oppose these crimes of aggression and crimes against the people of the US / World, no matter which War Criminal is currently occupying the White House. I really can't say this about too many "peace" groups, but I can iterate it strongly about St. Pete's for Peace!

After I returned to the Empire from a trip to Venezuela, I spoke at a "report back" in Marin County to its Latin American Solidarity committee and I was saying that, even though Chávez has accomplished much in his tenure, he knows he is not anywhere near completion.

So a Democrat in the back of the room asked me a somewhat valid question, "Obama has only been president for two and one half years; why don't you give him the patience you give Chávez?"

Well, because, according to the list above of Obama regime "accomplishments," there is one thing that I CANNOT say about Obama—that he doesn't know how to get things done.

He actually does know how to get things done. If he has the energy and political will to do so much harm, why can't he instead do good?

In the place of taking so much energy to passing a fascist health care bill that requires us to buy health insurance from private companies (and heftily taxes "Cadillac" plans), in the two years of a Democratic tyranny, why couldn't a universal single-payer plan have been legislated?

If he could spend billions of dollars, indeed wasting thousands for bombing at least six or seven countries at the present time, why couldn't he just as easily bring the troops home? Venezuela is bombing/occupying, um...let me see...ZERO countries.

It would have been easier to allow the provisions of the USA PATRIOT ACT to expire than it was to make most of the provisions permanent.

Money for education is being slashed at the federal, state, and local levels, and with little opportunity for jobs, more and more people cannot afford the extremely expensive education our colleges and universities offer. In 12 years Venezuela has brought literacy standards up to international measures by providing its citizens free education up through university. It seems like Obama is frightened of an educated populace, while Chávez knows one is essential to true, participatory government.

In closing, I would like to tell you a true story.

Once in 2006, I was called into MSNBC's Washington, DC studios to be on *HARDBALL* with Chris Matthews, but he had a guest-blabberer that day, Norah O'Donnell. Norah introduced me as the "woman who met with Communist Dictator, Hugo

Chávez." I then had to spend the rest of the show defending Chávez and the Revolution.

Finally, I guess Norah was getting tired of my precise answers and she asked me, "Would you rather have Hugo Chávez as your president than George Bush?"

(In my head) my answer was: "Is this a trick question? Of course I would," but I simply answered, "Yes."

If Hugo Chávez Frias were my president, my son would still be alive, for several reasons.

First of all, he wouldn't have had to choose between getting a university education and going into the most corrupt, diseased, and violent institution known to human history: the US military.

Secondly, Chávez has never invaded any other countries and millions of Iraqi, Afghans, etc. would be alive today if Chávez were my presidente.

Thirdly, I would have health care guaranteed as a human right and I would never have to worry about accident or illness ruining my finances, as well as my well-being.

Finally, instead of a growing gap between the rich and the poor, the trend would be diminishing—and no one person would control so much excess—we would be more, or less, the same.

A BETTER WORLD IS POSSIBLE, but we have to make it.

* * *

Acknowledgments

"Feeling gratitude and not expressing it is like wrapping a present and not giving it."
~ William Arthur Ward

I would like to thank so many people who make my work possible:

My Children who rarely complain about my constant "jet-setting" for peace;

My Grandchildren for giving me added motivation to participate in activism;

My readers and supporters who keep me ON the streets;

Eva Golinger for being such a dedicated revolutionary, friend of Cindy Sheehan's Soapbox and for writing the foreword to this book;

My daughter, Carly, for transcribing many of these interviews and giving me feedback;

To St. Pete's for Peace for keeping such a detailed account of the Obama regimes' crimes;

The people of Latin America, but especially of Venezuela and Cuba for being so kind to me and for profoundly living the struggle that we should be living in the States;

To all the people who generously gave of their time to be interviewed for this project;

To videographer, Clifford Bailey-Roddy, who traveled to Venezuela with me and filmed some of the footage for the documentary that will probably never be made;

To Michele Fergus for being a dedicated revolutionary book editor;

But, especially to Hugo Chávez for being such a brave and dedicated inspiration to me and to millions of people around the world who believe with all their hearts that a better world is possible!

SPONSORS FOR REVOLUTION, A LOVE STORY

Yoko Ono-Lennon

Melissa Beattie

George Cammarota

Linda J. Carraway

Sara Crawford

R. Bruce Denney

Ken Dolan-Del Vecchio

Carol J. Dutcher

John Everhart

Craig Fahan

Earl Gemert

Global Coalition for Peace

Stan Graves

Bromley Griffen

Martin Gugino

Irene Hadjipateras

John Heuer

Alfred Klinger

Marcia Leister

Laura Loper

Freeman Machado

Harold Mencher

Gregory Mucha

Clark Newhall

Craig Palmer

Donald Proud

Frank Scafani

Stephen K. Schuck

Joe Stokes

Ted Stolze

Marjorie Trifon

Robert Turner

Beth Shepherd

Lois Sturm

Kenneth Hughes

Carol Holland

Michael Rice

Jerilyn Tabor

Appendix

Why Socialism by Albert Einstein

Albert Einstein is the world-famous physicist. This article was originally published in the first issue of Monthly Review *(May 1949). It was subsequently published in May 1998 to commemorate the first issue of* Monthly Review's *50th year.*

Is it advisable for one who is not an expert on economic and social issues to express views on the subject of socialism? I believe for a number of reasons that it is.

Let us first consider the question from the point of view of scientific knowledge. It might appear that there are no essential methodological differences between astronomy and economics: scientists in both fields attempt to discover laws of general acceptability for a circumscribed group of phenomena in order to make the interconnection of these phenomena as clearly understandable as possible. But in reality such methodological differences do exist. The discovery of general laws in the field of economics is made difficult by the circumstance that observed economic phenomena are often affected by many factors which are very hard to evaluate separately. In addition, the experience which has accumulated since the beginning of the so-called civilized period of human history has—as is well known—been largely influenced and limited by causes which are by no means exclusively economic in nature. For example, most of the major states of history owed their existence to conquest. The conquering peoples established themselves, legally and economically, as the privileged class of the conquered country. They seized for themselves a monopoly of the land ownership and appointed a priesthood from among their own ranks. The priests, in control of education, made the class division of society into a permanent institution and created a system of values by which the people were thenceforth, to a large extent unconsciously, guided in their social behavior.

But historic tradition is, so to speak, of yesterday; nowhere have we really overcome what Thorstein Veblen called "the predatory phase" of human development. The observable economic facts belong to that phase and even such laws as we can derive from them are not applicable to other phases. Since the real purpose of socialism is precisely to overcome and advance beyond the predatory phase of human development, economic science in its present state can throw little light on the socialist society of the future.

Second, socialism is directed towards a social-ethical end. Science, however, cannot create ends and, even less, instill them in human beings; science, at most, can supply the means by which to attain certain ends. But the ends themselves are conceived by personalities with lofty ethical ideals and—if these ends are not stillborn, but vital and vigorous—are adopted and carried forward by those many human beings who, half unconsciously, determine the slow evolution of society.

For these reasons, we should be on our guard not to overestimate science and scientific methods when it is a question of human problems; and we should not assume that experts are the only ones who have a right to express themselves on questions affecting the organization of society.

Innumerable voices have been asserting for some time now that human society is passing through a crisis, that its stability has been gravely shattered. It is characteristic of such a situation that individuals feel indifferent or even hostile toward the group, small or large, to which they belong. In order to illustrate my meaning, let me record here a personal experience. I recently discussed with an intelligent and well-disposed man the threat of another war, which in my opinion would seriously endanger the existence of mankind, and I remarked that only a supra-national organization would offer protection from that danger. Thereupon my visitor, very calmly and coolly, said to me: "Why are you so deeply opposed to the disappearance of the human race?"

I am sure that as little as a century ago no one would have so lightly made a statement of this kind. It is the statement of a man who has striven in vain to attain an equilibrium within himself and has more or less lost hope of succeeding. It is the expression of a painful solitude and isolation from which so many people are suffering in these days. What is the cause? Is there a way out?

It is easy to raise such questions, but difficult to answer them with any degree of assurance. I must try, however, as best I can, although I am very conscious of the fact that our feelings and strivings are often contradictory and obscure and that they cannot be expressed in easy and simple formulas.

Man is, at one and the same time, a solitary being and a social being. As a solitary being, he attempts to protect his own existence and that of those who are closest to him, to satisfy his personal desires, and to develop his innate abilities. As a social being, he seeks to gain the recognition and affection of his fellow human beings, to share in their pleasures, to comfort them in their sorrows, and to improve their conditions of life. Only the existence of these varied, frequently conflicting, strivings accounts for the special character of a man, and their specific combination determines the extent to which an individual can achieve an inner equilibrium and can contribute to the well-being of society. It is quite possible that the relative strength of these two drives is, in the main, fixed by inheritance. But the personality that finally emerges is largely formed by the environment in which a man happens to find himself during his development, by the structure of the society in which he grows up, by the tradition of that society, and by its appraisal of particular types of behavior. The abstract concept "society" means to the individual human being the sum total of his direct and indirect relations to his contemporaries and to all the people of earlier generations. The individual is able to think, feel, strive, and work by himself; but he depends so much upon society—in his physical, intellectual, and emotional existence—that it is impossible to think of him, or to understand him, outside the framework of society. It is "society" which provides man with food, clothing, a home, the tools of work, language, the forms of thought, and most of the content of thought; his life is made possible through the labor and the accomplishments of the many millions past and present who are all hidden behind the small word "society."

It is evident, therefore, that the dependence of the individual upon society is a fact of nature which cannot be abolished—just as in the case of ants and bees. However, while the whole life process of ants and bees is fixed down to the smallest detail by rigid, hereditary instincts, the social pattern and interrelationships of human beings are very variable and susceptible to change. Memory, the capacity to make new combinations, the gift of oral communication, have made possible developments among human being which are not dictated by biological necessities. Such developments manifest themselves in traditions, institutions, and organizations; in literature; in scientific and engineering accomplishments; in works of art. This explains how it happens that, in a certain sense, man can influence his life through his own conduct, and that in this process conscious thinking and wanting can play a part.

Man acquires at birth, through heredity, a biological constitution which we must consider fixed and unalterable, including the natural urges which are characteristic of the human species. In addition, during his lifetime, he acquires a cultural constitution which he adopts from society through communication and through many other types of influences. It is this cultural constitution which, with the passage of time, is subject to change and which determines to a very large extent the relationship between the individual and society. Modern anthropology has taught us, through comparative investigation of so-called primitive cultures, that the social behavior of human beings may differ greatly, depending upon prevailing cultural patterns and the types of organization which predominate in society. It is on this that those who are striving to improve the lot of man may ground their hopes: human beings are not condemned, because of their biological constitution, to annihilate each other or to be at the mercy of a cruel, self-inflicted fate.

If we ask ourselves how the structure of society and the cultural attitude of man should be changed in order to make human life as satisfying as possible, we should constantly be conscious of the fact that there are certain conditions which we are unable to modify. As mentioned before, the biological nature of man is, for all practical purposes, not subject to change. Furthermore, technological and demographic developments of the last few centuries have created conditions which are here to stay. In relatively densely settled populations with the goods which are indispensable to their continued existence, an extreme division of labor and a highly-centralized productive apparatus are absolutely necessary. The time—which, looking back, seems so idyllic—is gone forever when individuals or relatively small groups could be completely self-sufficient. It is only a slight exaggeration to say that mankind constitutes even now a planetary community of production and consumption.

I have now reached the point where I may indicate briefly what to me constitutes the essence of the crisis of our time. It concerns the relationship of the individual to society. The individual has become more conscious than ever of his dependence upon society. But he does not experience this dependence as a positive asset, as an organic tie, as a protective force, but rather as a threat to his natural rights, or even to his economic existence. Moreover, his position in society is such that the egotistical drives of his make-up are constantly being accentuated, while his social drives, which are by nature weaker, progressively deteriorate. All human beings, whatever their position in society, are suffering from this process of deterioration. Unknowingly prisoners of their own egotism, they feel insecure, lonely, and deprived of the naive, simple, and unsophisticated enjoyment of life. Man can find meaning in life, short and perilous as it is, only through devoting himself to society.

The economic anarchy of capitalist society as it exists today is, in my opinion, the real source of the evil. We see before us a huge community of producers the members of which are unceasingly striving to deprive each other of the fruits of their collective labor—not by force, but on the whole in faithful compliance with legally established rules. In this respect, it is important to realize that the means of production—that is to say, the entire productive capacity that is needed for producing consumer goods as well as additional capital goods— may legally be, and for the most part are, the private property of individuals.

For the sake of simplicity, in the discussion that follows I shall call "workers" all those who do not share in the ownership of the means of production—although this does not quite correspond to the customary use of the term. The owner of the means of production is in a position to purchase the labor power of the worker. By using the means of production, the worker produces new goods which become the property of the capitalist. The essential point about this process is the relation between what the worker produces and what he is paid, both measured in terms of real value. Insofar as the labor contract is "free," what the worker receives is determined not by the real value of the goods he produces, but by his minimum needs and by the capitalists' requirements for labor power in relation to the number of workers competing for jobs. It is important to understand that even in theory the payment of the worker is not determined by the value of his product.

Private capital tends to become concentrated in few hands, partly because of competition among the capitalists, and partly because technological development and the increasing division of labor encourage the formation of larger units of production at the expense of smaller ones. The result of these developments is an oligarchy of private capital the enormous power of which cannot be effectively checked even by a democratically organized political society. This is true since the members of legislative bodies are selected by political parties, largely financed or otherwise influenced by private capitalists who, for all practical purposes, separate the electorate from the legislature. The consequence is that the representatives of the people do not in fact sufficiently protect the interests of the underprivileged sections of the population. Moreover, under existing conditions, private capitalists inevitably control, directly or indirectly, the main sources of information (press, radio, education). It is thus extremely difficult, and indeed in most cases quite impossible, for the individual citizen to come to objective conclusions and to make intelligent use of his political rights.

The situation prevailing in an economy based on the private ownership of capital is thus characterized by two main principles: first, means of production (capital) are privately owned and the owners dispose of them as they see fit; second, the labor contract is free. Of course, there is no such thing as a *pure* capitalist society in this sense. In particular, it should be noted that the workers, through long and bitter political struggles, have succeeded in securing a somewhat improved form of the "free labor contract" for certain categories of workers. But taken as a whole, the present day economy does not differ much from "pure" capitalism.

Production is carried on for profit, not for use. There is no provision that all those able and willing to work will always be in a position to find employment; an "army of unemployed" almost always exists. The worker is constantly in fear of losing his job. Since unemployed and poorly paid workers do not provide a profitable market, the production of consumers' goods is restricted, and great hardship is the consequence. Technological progress frequently results in more unemployment rather than in an easing of the burden of work for all. The profit motive, in conjunction with competition among capitalists, is responsible for an instability in the accumulation and utilization of capital which leads to increasingly severe depressions. Unlimited competition leads to a huge waste of labor, and to that crippling of the social consciousness of individuals which I mentioned before.

This crippling of individuals I consider the worst evil of capitalism. Our whole educational system suffers from this evil. An exaggerated competitive attitude is inculcated into the student, who is trained to worship acquisitive success as a preparation for his future career.

I am convinced there is only *one* way to eliminate these grave evils, namely through the establishment of a socialist economy, accompanied by an educational system which would be oriented toward social goals. In such an economy, the means of production are owned by society itself and are utilized in a planned fashion. A planned economy, which adjusts production to the needs of the community, would distribute the work to be done among all those able to work and would guarantee a livelihood to every man, woman, and child. The education of the individual, in addition to promoting his own innate abilities, would attempt to develop in him a sense of responsibility for his fellow men in place of the glorification of power and success in our present society.

Nevertheless, it is necessary to remember that a planned economy is not yet socialism. A planned economy as such may be accompanied by the complete enslavement of the individual. The achievement of socialism requires the solution of some extremely difficult socio-political problems: how is it possible, in view of the far-reaching centralization of political and economic power, to prevent bureaucracy from becoming all-powerful and overweening? How can the rights of the individual be protected and therewith a democratic counterweight to the power of bureaucracy be assured?

* * *

Clarity about the aims and problems of socialism is of greatest significance in our age of transition. Since, under present circumstances, free and unhindered discussion of these problems has come under a powerful taboo, I consider the foundation of this magazine to be an important public service.

Interview with Cynthia McKinney
(Continued from Chapter 9)

Sheehan: Absolutely, like you said, in 2000 all of these things occurred all over the country, but the focus was on Florida, and some of them, like the provisional ballot, were in place by 2004, but by then the damage had been done.

McKinney: The damage had been done.

And, if you look at—this is one of the things that I like to say is that in the 2004 election we had the introduction of the electronic voting machines.

Well, of course my home state of Georgia was the very first state to roll out these electronic voting machines from Diebold. The interesting thing is that approximately 80% of votes that are cast in the United States are cast on either Diebold or ES&S machines: these are electronic voting machines.

Interestingly, though, Diebold is founded by one Urosevich brother, and ES&S is founded by the other Urosevich brother. So basically you've got in the hands of one family 80% of vote counting in the United States. Isn't that amazing?

Now, in my 2006 election, I, well, the electronic voting machines broke down in the middle of the night, and of course I never regained the lead. But more than that, we were able to obtain affidavits from voters all over the state of Georgia who voted in my election. The interesting thing about that though is I only run in a district, a very compact, at that time, a very compact district.

Sheehan: But people from all over the state voted in your election, against you?

McKinney: Well we don't know because when we went to court to get the election data to see how those votes were counted, how they were treated, the court ruled that Diebold owned the election data.

Diebold is the electronic voting machine company and, even though it's a public contract paid for by taxpayers, they owned the election data. So there's no way to find out why the Fourth Congressional district race showed up on a screen in Atlanta, which is not in the fourth congressional district.

Sheehan: Were people able to vote in other districts, like were people in the fourth district able to vote in the third district races?

McKinney: We have no way of knowing exactly what happened because Diebold has the election data.

Sheehan: Just the affidavits from the people from other districts that say they voted in yours?

McKinney: That's exactly right, and we have people who voted for me, and we have people who voted against me, and they contacted us and said well, you know, we don't think it's right.

Sheehan: You're damn right it wasn't right.

McKinney: And when they called us and said I was in the run-off, they said well we voted for you in the primary but now you're not on the ballot for the run-off. We called those phantom votes, because they appeared one way but they disappeared in the run-off. And you know what the expert witnesses for the state said in court? That we have to "trust" them.

Sheehan: So, what you're saying is that the Secretary of State or the county Election Office does not own that data? The voting data—Diebold owns it?

McKinney: That's exactly what I'm saying. If you ask for the election data, then the county and the Secretary of State's office kicks the request over to Diebold and Diebold has the, since they own it, they have the discretion as to whether or not to turn that information over, and of course they say they can't turn it over because it's proprietary.

Sheehan: Wow, wow, no, it sounds like it's public information!

McKinney: It should be public information, and then on top of all of that, what we have are poor election administrators. They don't know when a machine is malfunctioning during the voting process or not, so you could have a machine that is not even calibrated at zero at the beginning of the day. You have these machines that are vulnerable to hacking. You could walk in with a Blackberry and do a little this and that and you can change the vote tabulation literally right there.

At the end of the day the machines are all hooked up to telephone lines. Now guess what, telephone lines allow the hacking to occur as well. I've participated with Bev Harris in several experiments where literally before our eyes we saw the election data change the tabulation because of outside interference.

Now, if we add to that a very real situation that happened in 2004, and that is that in the presidential election, the vote counting and tabulation took place on Republican owned machines. So, if you privatize your democracy, then you've basically placed the right of representation and the right of self-determination in the hands of private corporations. That is what the people of the United States have done.

Sheehan: It sounds not like a democracy but fascism.

McKinney: And the Democratic Party is part and parcel of the problem because even though they have a majority and have had a majority since 2007 they have done nothing to insure election integrity.

Sheehan: Right, and also, in Florida in 2000 and Ohio in 2004 the Secretaries of State were both chairmen of the Republican parties in their separate states.

McKinney: That's exactly right, so in Ohio you had the man, Blackwell, and in Florida you had Catherine Harris, and I served with her in the House, and she was rewarded for stealing the election with a Congressional seat. Because I did an investigation to expose, you know we brought Choice Points Vice president in and made him swear, then that's how we found out just exactly the mechanism they use, and in fact, as I recall, what the VP told us was that the State of Florida asked for an inaccurate list—they asked Choice Point to give them a list that wasn't accurate so they could have the discretion to deny rightfully registered people the right to vote. It's all a plan.

Sheehan: Yeah, for sure, and you know, they're just playing these games with people's lives.

McKinney: Yes, they are. Choice Point was also involved in the election theft in Mexico, so that the correct choice of the Mexican people was denied the opportunity to serve as the head of state. And instead they put Calderon in there who was supposed to deliver the electricity grid and Pemex, the oil, Pemex an oil company over to US corporations. But when they're election was stolen, Mexico city was shut down for six months and they formed a shadow government and that shadow government held elections and did everything

Sheehan: Yes, they called it the "legitimate government," but when our elections are stolen we just go, "Oh well. That's the way things go." I really admire the people of Mexico; I think they're really radical.

Well, speaking of Mexico, Venezuela also votes on voting machines. However, when they vote the person gets a receipt. The person checks the receipt and makes sure everything that he or she voted for is correct, and then it goes into a ballot box to be audited if there's a need for that. You know, even if it's not the ideal system, it's better than the system in place in many places in the United States.

In 2000 and 2004, voter fraud is well documented, it's not a conspiracy theory. In Ohio there were things that happened that were statistically impossible, but of course we don't believe in statistics or science in the US, we believe in myths, we believe in fairy tales, but what happened in 2008? Was that election stolen, you know, are our elections only stolen if a Republican wins? Or because we know most of these people who do election protection or integrity are progressives, or Democrats? So in 2008, I believe Obama got 52% and I believe McCain got around 47%, so what happened? And in this answer I want you to include what you found out in that COINTELPRO document about what was promulgated in 1965.

McKinney: In 2000, we saw election fraud that was by means other than electronic voting machines. In 2004, we saw election fraud by means of electronic voting machines and other means as well. And nothing happened to change the platform on which elections are administered in our country for the 2008 election; in fact, the insidious proprietary voting machinery was used even more widely, so therefore, if nothing was done to improve the situation, everything remains the same.

So, honestly, for the 2008 election, we can say the black vote was probably severely undercounted, as it always is. We could say that there were other votes, white votes as well, that were not counted, and therefore we still do not have an accurate count, which is the will of the people

Sheehan: In that year in Ohio, we heard that they'd bring in two machines...

McKinney: ...And you'd have 1500 people voting in that precinct

Sheehan: And long lines, and in white communities there'd be like 8 or 10 machines you know, no lines, so you know, besides them controlling the machines they still do stuff like that, but in '08 we don't hear about that, not one thing.

McKinney: Well we had a situation that arose in Georgia where one of our constitutional officers was on the verge of really stopping the election because of the vote flipping that was going with the voting machines in Georgia. Now can you imagine deploying a machine that can't function in the heat, and in Georgia you've got 70% humidity and 90 degrees and the machines break down because of the heat. But then that particular constitutional officer was pulled off the election, so if you get the desired result, you really don't complain.

But really the desired result ought to be an accurate reflection of the will of the people, that's why we go to vote, and that's called self-determination. Anything that diminishes what we know the will of the people is is a diminishment of our right to self-determination, and that's a human right. And our rights are being diminished literally right before our eyes and the people who we entrust with the responsibility to look out for our interest, they really are shirking their responsibility and the only people who suffer in the end are the ones that really count.

Sheehan: And we know in 2000 Al Gore didn't fight for the people, we know yourself and the black caucus were just so upset about that and tried really hard to see that all votes were counted, not just black votes, but Al Gore...

McKinney: ...Al Gore told Barbara Boxer who was inclined to provide the additional two hours so we could have the debate about what had happened in Florida, he told her, you know, just let it slide.

Sheehan: Right, and there's the famous footage in Fahrenheit 911 *of you guys begging Al Gore and...*

McKinney: ...And he's presiding and ruling us out of order as we're trying to fight for him.

Sheehan: Right, and you weren't fighting for him...

McKinney: ...Right, we were fighting for the people.

Sheehan: And in '04 Kerry just like totally caved in, he left the campaign...

McKinney: ...he lost before he even began the campaign, that was one of the most ludicrous examples of someone running, he said, "Sure just put my name on the ballot," that was a disservice to the people. You see, in the South, we have a little bit different view of things because down here we are accustomed to fighting the Democratic Party, because at the time of my birth the Democratic Party was a white-only party, that was their law, and if a white person wanted to participate in politics, they had to be a Republican, so we see things differently.

When the Democratic Party became the party of hope for black people, then we gave all of our hope over to that party, and that was during the Civil Rights struggle. It had begun before that, with the Franklin Roosevelt Administration, with the issuance of jobs and that sort of thing, but really it was during the Civil Rights movement, and there were real victories that, well, we were actually fighting the Democrats, because the Democrats in the south were Dixiecrats, they were boll weevils, they were the solid South, and the solid South at that time was a South against the idea of black voting.

So really this idea of black people being so wedded to the abusive spousal relationship to the Democrats, who are still sending their children off to die in war, who are still giving money to bankers who really don't need it, who are investing their hopes in a Social Security system and a Medicare system, but black people don't even live long enough to take advantage of these programs.

For us, to invest all of our hope in a political party that has a multitude of interests, and ours come last on the totem pole, is really quite politically dysfunctional, and then we have the rise of a black candidate that talks about hope.

* * *

"The Bolivarian Revolution is a Beacon of Light"
Cindy Sheehan's Interview with Angela Davis

Welcome back to Cindy Sheehan's soapbox. As I said before the break, my special guest today is Angela Davis.

She is an American socialist, philosopher, political activist, and retired professor with the History of Consciousness Department at the University of Santa Cruz. She was the Director of the University's Feminine Studies Department.

Davis was largely active during the Civil Rights Movement and was associated with the Black Panthers. Her interests are in feminism, African American studies, critical theories, Marxism, popular music, social consciousness, and the philosophy and history of punishment and prisons.

She wrote about the FBI and its targeting of the Black Panther Party as a part of its counter-intelligence program, COINTELPRO.

Angela was tried and acquitted of suspected involvement in the Soledad Brothers' August 1970 abduction and murder of Judge Harold Haley in Marin County California—even though she had purchased the weapons involved, had written letters to one of the prisoners, escaped, and became a fugitive from the law after the murders.

Angela Davis was twice a candidate for vice president on the Communist Party, USA ticket during the Reagan era.

Since moving in the early 1990s from party communism to other forms of political commitment she has identified herself as a Democratic Socialist.

Davis is the founder of *Critical Resistance*, an organization working to abolish the Prison Industrial Complex. She was on the FBI's 10 most wanted list for a time.

Angela Davis, there is so much confusion between the terms Capitalism, socialism and communism. Can you briefly compare and contrast the philosophies?

Davis: Perhaps I will begin with capitalism.

Capitalism is an economic system that is based on the production of profit at the expense of the workers who actually produce the products.

In many ways you can say capitalism is based on a trick and that trick involves the assumption that workers get paid for what they do. But in actuality, as Marx pointed our many years ago, they are getting paid for their capacity to work, their ability to work, and the difference between what they actually produce and what they get paid is called: profit.

Marx's definition is the nature of exploitation. It really has nothing to do with a moral judgment against Capitalists. It's simply the way the Capitalist system works.

Those who already have the capital exploit those who have nothing to sell but their labor power. Then as we move on, socialism is a system that is not based on the production of profit, but rather based on the satisfaction of peoples' needs, the fulfillment of social needs.

Therefore, in a socialist system it would make no sense at all for there to be profit generated from health care. Because health care would be considered a right, health care would be free, and education would be free and housing would cost very little: Housing would be subsidized by the government.

Then communism I would categorize as the ultimate stage of socialism.

Of course, it's been said, using Marx words, socialism is "from each according to his or her ability and each according to his or her works."

And communism would be "from each according to his or her ability to each according to his or her needs."

That is to say that everyone in a Communist society would have all of their basic needs fulfilled regardless of what their profession is or regardless of whether they are unemployed.

Sheehan: Does a socialist system lead to communism?

Davis: Well, I would like to think just as capitalism was or is a moment in history that should be transcended; capitalism demonstrates needs can be satisfied. It demonstrates the amazing productive power that can be generated by the workers.

Unfortunately, that is subordinated to profit. So socialism would use that productive power to begin to satisfy people's needs.

And, in the beginning, one would have a system in which certain things would not cost. But other things would.

In the end, one would think that society would be structured so that everyone's needs could be fulfilled—So that someone who is disabled would not have to worry about where to get money to attend school or health care.

Yeah, I'm an optimist and I think we still need to move in that direction, at least so far, in our vision for the future. We should think about countries like Cuba where they have demonstrated that it is possible to build a society in which health care, education, and housing are not subject to profit for the profit motive.

Sheehan: What do you think of Venezuela's Bolivarian Revolution?

Davis: I think that the Bolivarian Revolution under Hugo Chávez in Venezuela is really a beacon of light—not only for all of Latin America, but for the entire hemisphere.

They have demonstrated in Venezuela that it is possible to begin to build a different kind of society—just as Cuba has held out for all of these years. I can remember the Cuban Revolution and the triumph of the Cuban Revolution.

I was in high school, so we are talking about 1959, 1960 and here we are in the 21st century and the Cuban Revolution continues to persevere.

That is very exciting to see the developments in Venezuela— particularly the sensitivity to people who have little, the poor people, working class people.

And the way in which the abundance of oil in Venezuela is being used to fulfill people's needs and not to generate profit for corporations, like BP, who were then responsible for polluting the ocean and for destroying marine life.

It's a real breath of fresh air. For those if us who consider ourselves socialists or communists for a long time, it has demonstrated that indeed our lives were worthwhile.

Sheehan: We hear a lot that President Obama is a socialist— especially from the right end of the political spectrum. What do you think about that Angela Davis? Is Obama a socialist?

Davis: Well, of course, unfortunately, what we have seen over the last couple of years since Obama took office is the resurgence of a really vitriolic rightwing resistance, and they have learned how to use the old communist tactics in very vicious ways.

When I first heard these claims that Obama was a socialist, I thought, "Well, it would really be wonderful if Obama were a socialist." But, unfortunately, it is in the same tradition as those who called Martin Luther King, Jr. a "socialist."

I think if we didn't have that anti-communist pressure from the right it would be possible for there to be a more effective movement in the direction of socialism.

Sheehan: Angela, what are your thoughts on so called 21st century socialism?

Davis: I do think that we need to think in terms of a 21st century socialist movement in the United States of America. Otherwise we assume that capitalism is our future.

Since the dismantling of socialist nations in the early '90s there has been this assumption that capitalism is triumphant, that capitalism is here, and will be eternally present in our lives. That's very sad if we have to think of our future in terms of exploitation.

It's not only the economic dimension of capitalism that is so destructive; it's the ideological dimension that is destructive as well. Capitalism posits the individual as the basic unit of society and to think of a future of individuals fighting to become more powerful Capitalists is very, very sad.

We have to be able to imagine a future in which community means a great deal to us, in which there is solidarity, in which there is care for those that are less fortunate, in which education is not a commodity, in which a society in which every one has the right to education, and health care, and housing and jobs. So I am holding out for that. I have been struggling since I was a teenager. I guess I might say that I have been struggling too long to give up now.

Sheehan: Here in the United States definitely a stigma is attached to the word "socialism." Can you explain that?

Davis: The word "socialism" has such a stigma attached to it because of the media pundits. The rightwing politicians have been able to draw on the old anti-communism—the notion that communism denotes an evil empire—the idea that it is an anathema to democracy.

What impresses me, however, is that young people are not always persuaded by the rightwing rhetoric. A recent survey by the Pew Center indicates that young people especially think of capitalism (almost a majority) in negative terms and socialism in more positive terms.

So I think that people are not always incapable of seeing through the lies, and the deceit, and the fraudulent representation of socialism.

Many people are starting to recognize that we need an alternative to capitalism that thrives on racism, that thrives on exploitation, that has polluted the environment and cares for nothing aside from the amount of money that can be generated from any given project. And it doesn't care for the future.

Capitalists don't even mind the fact that there may be no planet available in the coming generations—they're only interested in the profit that is available in the moment. No sense of history—no sense of past history—no sense of future history.

I suppose I would conclude by saying that I learned long ago that history is really important; that we think of ourselves as agents of history, that we think of ourselves as products of history. And, as a matter of fact, capitalism is a product of history. It came into being in history. And if it came into being in history, it should probably go out of existence in history as well.

Sheehan: Angela Davis, as a lifelong teacher do you have a message for young people?

Davis: Well, Jose Marti, who was one of the heroes of the Cuban revolution once said that children, our youth, are the future and hope of the world.

My message to young people would be that they follow their sense of adventure—that they follow their need for creativity. Because all of the wonderful things we experience today have been visions and ideas of young people at one point or another.

And I always say, as we grow older, we have to learn that it is the young people who have the new ideas. In that sense, we have to learn to follow their leadership when we are talking about the anti-war movement and the need to end the war in Afghanistan, as well as Iraq.

When we are talking about anti-racism and the importance of generating a movement that recognized the extent to which structural racism is still a part of our lives here. Particularly with the Prison Industrial Complex given the more than 2 million people who are behind bars, the majority of whom are people of color. And in all these movements I see young people taking the decisive steps.

Sheehan: What are your thoughts on the dominant two-party political system here in the United States?

Davis: Well my sense has been for a very long time that the two-party system constricts any real imagination, and as long as we have a Democratic Party and a Republican Party, of course that are tied to corporate interests, capitalist corporate interests, we are never going to be able to move beyond those capitalist interests.

So as independent politics, I can say many of us voted for Obama. I voted for Obama and I can say it is probably the first time I voted for a Democrat, because I have always voted for the Communist, the Socialist, the Peace and Freedom Party candidates or the Green party candidate.

So I think that today more than ever before we have the first African-American in office. We need to emphasize independent politics, we need to emphasize 3rd party politics, we need to emphasize a more radical political vision than would ever be possible under the auspices of the Democratic Party.

Sheehan: Angela Davis, do you have anything else you would like to add for my readers?

Davis: Well, I suppose the only other thing I would say is that it is so important for people, particularly in the US, to question the representation of the dominant media. It is impossible to understand fully. It is impossible to understand what is going on in Venezuela if we rely on CNN, if we rely on the dominant media forces—and to consult independent media. Consult progressive media.

What's happening in Venezuela is so exciting and it would be wonderful if more people in this country could even participate in that excitement and then begin to imagine what it might be like to transform the United States of America in accordance with a socialist project.

Sheehan: This interview was made in September of 2010.

Thanks to Angela Davis for her work, dignity, and time, and thanks to Dede Miller for transcribing the interview!

President Chávez's Letter to the UN on Palestinian Statehood

Miraflores, September 17, 2011

His Excellency, Ban Ki-moon, Secretary General of the United Nations

Mr. Secretary General:

Distinguished representatives of the peoples of the world:

I address these words to the United Nations General Assembly, to this great forum that represents all the people of earth, to ratify, on this day and in this setting, Venezuela's full support of the recognition of the Palestinian State: of Palestine's right to become a free, sovereign, and independent state. This represents an act of historic justice towards a people who carry with them, from time immemorial, all the pain and suffering of the world.

In his memorable essay The Grandeur of Arafat, the great French philosopher Gilles Deleuze wrote with the full weight of the truth: The Palestinian cause is first and foremost the set of injustices that these people have suffered and continue to suffer. And I dare add that the Palestinian cause also represents a constant and unwavering will to resist, already written in the historic memory of the human condition. A will to resist that is born of the most profound love for the earth. Mahmoud Darwish, the infinite voice of the longed-for Palestine, with heartfelt conscience speaks about this love: We don't need memories/ because we carry within us Mount Carmelo/ and in our eyelids is the herb of Galilee./ Don't say: If only we could flow to my country like a river!/ Don't say that!/ Because *we are in the flesh of our country/ and our country is in our flesh.*

Against those who falsely assert that what has happened to the Palestinian people is not genocide, Deleuze himself states with unfaltering lucidity: From beginning to end, it involved acting as if the Palestinian people not only must not exist, but had never existed. It represents the very essence of genocide: to decree that a people do not exist; to deny them the right to existence.

In this regard, the great Spanish writer Juan Goytisolo is quite right when he forcefully states: The biblical promise of the land of Judea and Samaria to the tribes of Israel is not a notarized property contract that authorizes the eviction of those who were born and live on that land. This is precisely why conflict resolution in the Middle East must, necessarily, bring justice to the Palestinian people; this is the only path to peace.

It is upsetting and painful that the same people who suffered one of the worst examples of genocide in history have become the executioners of the Palestinian people: it is upsetting and painful that the heritage of the Holocaust be the Nakba. And it is truly disturbing that Zionism continues to use the charge of anti-Semitism as blackmail against those who oppose their violations and crimes. Israel has, blatantly and despicably, used and continues to use the memory of the victims. And they do so to act with complete impunity against Palestine. It's worth mentioning that anti-Semitism is a Western, European, scourge in which the Arabs do not participate. Furthermore, let's not forget that it is the Semite Palestine people who suffer from the ethnic cleansing practiced by the Israeli colonialist State.

I want to make myself clear: It is one thing to denounce anti-Semitism, and an entirely different thing to passively accept that Zionistic barbarism enforces an apartheid regime against the Palestinian people. From an ethical standpoint those who denounce the first, must condemn the second.

A necessary digression: it is frankly abusive to confuse Zionism with Judaism. Throughout time we have been reminded of this by several Jewish intellectuals such as Albert Einstein and Erich Fromm. And today there are an ever increasing number of conscientious citizens, within Israel itself, who openly oppose Zionism and its criminal and terrorist practices.

We must spell it out: Zionism, as a world vision, is absolutely racist. Irrefutable proof of this can be seen in these words written with terrifying cynicism by Golda Meir: How are we to return the occupied territories? There is nobody to return them to. There is no such thing as a Palestinian people. It is not as people think, that there existed a people called Palestinians, who considered themselves as Palestinians, and that we came and threw them out and took their country. They didn't exist."

It is important to remember that: from the end of the 19th century, Zionism called for the return of the Jewish people to Palestine and the creation of a national state of its own. This approach was beneficial for French and British colonialism, as it would later be for Yankee imperialism. The West has always encouraged and supported the Zionist occupation of Palestine by military means.

Read and reread the document historically known as the Balfour Declaration of 1917: the British Government assumed the legal authority to promise a national home in Palestine to the Jewish people, deliberately ignoring the presence and wishes of its inhabitants. It should be added that Christians and Muslims lived in peace for centuries in the Holy Land up until the time when Zionism began to claim it as its complete and exclusive property.

Let's not forget that beginning in the second decade of the 20th century, Zionism started to develop its expansionist plans by taking advantage of the colonial British occupation of Palestine. By the end of World War II, the Palestinian people's tragedy worsened, with their expulsion from their territory and, at the same time, from history. In 1947, the despicable and illegal UN resolution 181 recommends dividing Palestine into a Jewish State, an Arab State, and an area under international control (Jerusalem and Belem). Shamefully, 56 percent of the territory was granted to Zionism to establish its State. In fact, this resolution violated international law and blatantly ignored the will of the vast Arab majority: the right to self-determination of the people became a dead letter.

From 1948 to date, the Zionist State has continually applied its criminal strategy against the Palestinian people with the constant support of its unconditional ally, the United States of America. This unconditional allegiance is clearly observed by the fact that Israel directs and sets US international policy for the Middle East. That's why the great Palestinian and universal conscience Edward Said stated that any peace agreement built on the alliance with the United States would be an alliance that confirms Zionist power, rather than one that confronts it.

Now then: contrary to what Israel and the United States are trying to make the world believe through transnational media outlets, what happened and continues to happen in Palestine — using Said's words— is not a religious conflict, but a political conflict, with a colonial and imperialist stamp. It did not begin in the Middle East, but rather in Europe.

What was and continues to be at the heart of the conflict? Debate and discussion has prioritized Israel's security while ignoring Palestine's. This is corroborated by recent events; a good example is the latest act of genocide set off by Israel during its Operation Molten Lead in Gaza.

Palestine's security cannot be reduced to the simple acknowledgement of a limited self-government and self-policing in its "enclaves" along the west bank of the Jordan and in the Gaza Strip. This ignores the creation of the Palestinian State, in the borders set prior to 1967 with East Jerusalem as its capital; and the rights of its citizens and their self-determination as a people. This further disregards the compensation and subsequent return to the Homeland of 50 percent of the Palestinian people who are scattered all over the world, as established by resolution 194.

It's unbelievable that a country (Israel) that owes its existence to a general assembly resolution could be so disdainful of the resolutions that emanate from the UN, said Father Miguel D'Escoto when pleading for the end of the massacre against the people of Gaza in late 2008 and early 2009.

Mr. Secretary General and distinguished representatives of the peoples of the world:

It is impossible to ignore the crisis in the United Nations. In 2005, before this very same General Assembly, we argued that the United Nations model had become exhausted. The fact that the debate on the Palestinian issue has been delayed and is being openly sabotaged reconfirms this.

For several days, Washington has been stating that, at the Security Council, it will veto what will be a majority resolution of the General Assembly: the recognition of Palestine as a full member of the UN. In the Statement of Recognition of the Palestinian State, Venezuela, together with the sister Nations that make up the Bolivarian Alliance for the Peoples of Our America (ALBA), have denounced that such a just aspiration could be blocked by this means. As we know, the empire, in this and other instances, is trying to impose its double standard on the world stage: Yankee double standards are violating international law in Libya, while allowing Israel to do whatever it pleases, thus becoming the main accomplice of the Palestinian genocide being carried out by the hands of Zionist barbarity. Edward Said touched a nerve when he wrote that: Israeli interests in the United States have made the US' Middle East policy Israeli-centric.

I would like to conclude with the voice of Mahmoud Darwish in his memorable poem On This Earth: We have on this earth what makes life worth living: On this earth, the lady of earth, Mother of all beginnings/ Mother of all ends. She was called... Palestine./ Her name later became... Palestine./ My Lady, because you are my Lady, I deserve life.

It will continue to be called Palestine: Palestine will live and overcome! Long-live free, sovereign and independent Palestine!

Hugo Chávez Frías

President of the Bolivarian Republic of Venezuela

***

The Soapbox: Transcript July 24, 2011 with Eva Golinger

President Chávez is pretty adamant about the fact that Venezuela is no longer a colony of the US.

President Hugo Chávez of Venezuela

Sheehan: A lot of my friends and contacts and fans of the show have been asking me how President Chávez of Venezuela has been since he had a recent battle with cancer. So we're going to bring on the expert of all things Venezuelan, our good friend, Eva Golinger.

Eva welcome back to Cindy Sheehan's Soapbox.

Golinger: Thank you so much, Cindy.

Sheehan: Well we always want to have you on whenever there is a lot of concern or things happening in Venezuela. I have so many fans of the show, supporters, and contacts who have been very concerned about the health of Chávez. Can you give us an update on that?

Golinger: Well, President Chávez is currently undergoing chemotherapy treatment.

He is in Cuba where his initial cancer was detected in a very unexpected way.

I guess nobody ever expects it and he, of course, certainly didn't. I mean Chávez is very young. He is almost 57 years old and he's never had any major health problems. There's not cancer in his family that is known, so it wasn't an issue that was of concern in terms of his health.

However, he is someone who works incredibly hard. He's been in office 12 years, elected twice, and works nonstop. Has never taken a vacation, doesn't take sick days, and is incredibly dedicated and committed to his work. That has sort of been his rhythm for the past decade or so. Now it has caught up with him. It's taken a toll on his ability to continue that level of work that he has been doing as President of Venezuela.

When the cancer was detected initially, which was in June, about mid-June, what was found was a pelvic abscess, which was immediately drained, and after the infection subsided they found a mass of malignant cancer cells and that was immediately removed. It was a very intense operation that took six and a half hours. You can imagine that level of surgery, you know, the cutting through all of his muscles—just the type of wound he had after that. So since that time, which was the

20th of June, he's been recovering from that and waiting to be able to have another revision done, a thorough revision of his body, and to start the chemo.

So the latest update, which Chávez made public himself, that no further cancer cells have been detected in his body, so the tumor was taken out in it's entirety and nothing seems to have been left behind. Of course, the chemotherapy treatments are a precaution to prevent the cancer from coming back. So that's what he's doing.

He delegated some of his administrative functions to the Executive Vice President and the (?), and to the Minister of Finance and Planning Jorge Giordani. But it is really administrative in nature and Chávez remains at the head of government.

They activated an electronic signature when he left for Cuba so he can himself still sign documents and he's regularly involved, in Venezuela.

Cindy, Twitter is a real big deal. Chávez is one of the leading Tweeters and everyday since he has been in Cuba he has been tweeting several times a day starting in the early morning hours because now he is getting up at five in the morning so he is sending out Tweets from that time on and throughout the day. And, you know, it makes people feel and believe that of course he is following everything that is going on and he is still fully capacitated to remain as President.

Sheehan: Well, there is always, well not always, but for quite a while there's been a very active opposition to the revolution and the administration of President Chávez. How is the opposition trying to take advantage of this illness?

Golinger: Well it's really grotesque. From the beginning, first they were really doubting that he was diagnosed with cancer, was sick, thought it was a ploy, a strategy for his reelection.

Venezuela has presidential elections in 2012 so the campaigns, some of them have already been started. President Chávez's candidacy has already been launched by his party the PSUV, and so the opposition were trying to make up stories, myths, and rumors speculating about his health. One saying that it was false, and then the other side saying he was terminally ill and going to be out of the picture soon, which isn't true either.

And, on top of that, there has been external aid to try to urge opposition figures, groups, and organizations to try and promote a climate of chaos and destabilization in order to permit another coup d'état to be executed against President Chávez and, in fact, just this week the *Miami Herald* Spanish language version, the *Nuevo Herald*, published a front page article basically calling on the opposition to organize conditions for a coup and also asking for help from the US government to assure that it happens and is successful, saying that this is the time to take advantage of the situation, take advantage of Chávez's weakness and execute the coup before it is too late.

You know, making up all kinds of stories about session, that Chávez is preparing a double. I mean they are really fantasizing about things that are not happening and that have never happened. This has been an ongoing situation in Venezuela with an unfortunate opposition that has not been willing to work within the framework of democracy.

So that's what has been going on and, at the same time, there is another sector of the opposition saying, "Well, since Chávez is sick and undergoing treatment that he should just be inhabilitated from being President and should delegate all his power and authority to the Vice President who should temporarily take over." Which is ridiculous because Chávez is not incapacitated mentally and he is fully in front of government affairs and involved in everything as he always has been and will continue to be.

They have also been trying to say his absence from the country, which has been authorized by the Parliament, the National Assembly, is something illegal, even though it is not, since it's been authorized in a legal way. But the opposition says, "Well he is out of the country, so he's not governing so, therefore, there's a power vacuum." Which isn't true either.

It's not the first time. I would remind our listeners, for example, that US President Reagan had three cancers during his Presidency. He underwent major surgery for colon cancer right before he was reelected in 1985. There's some evidence to show that his treatments and surgeries were conducted in Germany. So they didn't even take place in the United States. So it's not unusual.

There have been several times when presidents in Latin America, for example, recently the President of Paraguay, Fernando Lugo, had lymphatic cancer and he's been cured and that was recently while he was in the Presidency, he still is. Then Brazil's President, Dilma Rousseff, also had the same type of cancer. Before she was elected President she underwent treatment and was successfully elected President.

So the treatments are out there as long as you catch it before it is too late which is what appears to be the case with President Chávez. He should fully recover and there is no reason why the opposition should try to convince public opinion internationally that Chávez isn't governing and that there is a power vacuum.

Sheehan: Has there been any response from the US about his illness or the calls about helping to overthrow his government?

Golinger: Well, the United States government is being incredibly cautious in this scenario. Chávez is considered a foe by the State Department particularly, but by, of course, all of the US government. So they're playing this one pretty slowly, patiently looking at the scenario, seeing what's going on and, besides, that's in the public light.

In terms of what is going on behind the scenes, I would say certainly there are efforts and negotiations going on with the opposition groups the US has been funding now for years with US tax payer dollars. Trying to promote Chávez's overthrow. So yeah, I mean certainly there is a sort of unspoken encouragement of anything that could remove Chávez from power.

The fact that the *Miami Herald* was citing Roger Noriega, who is a known figure very closely linked to the US government now for decades and was part of the Bush administration, a part of the Reagan administration. Unfortunately, even though he has incredibly ridiculous concepts of what is happening in Latin America, he tends to have influence over those in power. So he is one of the ones who has been calling directly for Chávez's overthrow now that Chávez has been diagnosed with cancer in saying that the US government should immediately send support, not just financially, but militarily to insure that that happens.

Sheehan: What would be the difference between that and the US involvement in Libya right now?

Golinger: Well there's really not much difference, I mean the case in Libya is outrageous. The fact that not only did a bombing campaign begin against a country that wasn't a threat to anybody else, in terms of being a threat to a foreign nation. Those nations that have been attacking it and bombing it now for months. But, on top of that, when the US government and NATO allies were unable to kill Gadhaffi, basically assassinate Gadhaffi, which was the overall objective, or invoke regime change. Now they're installing an illegitimate parallel government.

So those are the types of scenarios that are incredibly dangerous precedents being set today that can be used or applied to other countries like Venezuela. I would just remind listeners again that Venezuela has the largest oil reserves in the world and it has just been recertified again by OPEC, the Organization of Oil Producing Countries, that Venezuela is number one in terms of oil reserves, so this of course makes it a huge target of the world's most powerful interests.

Sheehan: There are similar cases and parallels between Libya and Venezuela in that both of the countries use their wealth, their natural resources, and oil wealth to improve the lives of their citizens, and that means that the US oil companies and British companies can't reap most of the profits like they did before Chávez was elected in Venezuela in 1998.

Golinger: That's absolutely correct.

A lot of people don't actually know that Libya has the highest standard of living of all the African nations. Without passing judgment on his government there have been policies that have invested in social well-being over decades now.

In the case of Venezuela, it is new under the Chávez administration over the past decade—these policies of using oil profits to invest back into the people, invest back into the infrastructure and development of the country. And as of right now a normal expected rate of income from oil sales Venezuela invests, the government—because obviously the oil is nationalized—the government invests 60 percent of all profits directly into social programs relating to health care, education, housing initiatives, and job training programs. Then there was a new windfall tax law enacted last year which, because of increasing oil prices, says that basically if oil is over 90 dollars a barrel, which it is right now, then 90 percent of oil profits coming into Venezuela are going to be invested into social programs.

So it really is a majority of the money coming in that is being used to invest back into the people and it has had a tremendous effect. Poverty has been reduced in Venezuela by over 50 percent in the past decade. That's an immense change right there.

We have universal free accessible health care for everybody. No one is asked for insurance cards, or turned away, or left to die if they can't afford to pay for health care, because there are free quality clinics everywhere that have just been built in the last few years.

Education at all levels is accessible and it's free, you know, public education. The same goes for a whole wide variety of programs, including super markets that have subsidized products to combat inflation speculation from the private markets, which is a big problem in Venezuela.

Obviously that is something that is not seen in any way as favorable to multinationals and foreign interests. Especially because in the case of Venezuela there have been strict controls implemented on multinationals in Venezuela over the past decade that existed before but were never really implemented—such as making foreign corporations that are involved in the oil industry pay taxes and royalties on their profits. Things that are normal anywhere else, in Venezuela, which operated as a US colony, those types of initiatives were never implemented before, now they are.

Now companies operating in Venezuela have to abide by the law. It's pretty straight-forward, as long as they are willing to do it. But when they were used to acting above the law, of course then they reacted to these types of policies and it is not convenient to powerful interests that try to exploit and basically take as much as they can get out of resource wealthy nations like Venezuela.

Sheehan: Well was that one of the reasons for the first coup attempt in April of 2002? I hope it was the first and only coup attempt. I don't want to seem like there is another one coming. But right before it happened, didn't the national assembly pass laws to nationalize more of the oil production and profits from it under the national oil company in Venezuela?

Golinger: Yeah, that is correct. Oil was nationalized in Venezuela in 1976, so way before Chávez became president. After he was in office and there was a whole initiative for constitutional reform under a new constitution that was drafted and ratified under the national referendum by everyone in Venezuela eligible to vote.

New laws were implemented and one of those related to hydrocarbons, the oil industry, was dealing with what I was just talking about in terms of making sure that foreign companies operating in Venezuela are paying their royalties, are paying their taxes, cannot have more than a 49 percent share in any kind of joint venture with Venezuela's state oil companies. Otherwise it wouldn't be a nationalized product if foreign nationals can have higher stakes than the national company. So, yeah, there was a restructuring of the industry that affected foreign interests, as well as those nationally of the Venezuelan elite—the economic elite that were running the industry like a private company, pocketing most of the products and embezzling them outside of the country to buy their big homes throughout Miami and New York and the Caribbean Islands. So, actually, right before the coup took place in April 2002 President Chávez had changed the entire board of Directors of PDVSA, which is the state oil company. That was sort of the straw that broke the camel's back. That set things finally into motion that had been building up anyway, with support from the US, of course, and other interested parties in terms of trying to get Chávez out of power.

What Chávez did, in fact, was once he was back in office after the coup was defeated by the people of Venezuela and he was rescued and returned to power to his legitimate office, he reinstated the board of directors in an attempt to reconcile and extend an olive branch to the opposition—Which was a giant mistake because they weren't looking to reconcile or work with them. They were looking to get him out of office no matter what.

Months after the coup, and after he reinstated the board back to PDVSA, they initiated a very extensive and very economically damaging strike on the oil industry, where they basically shut it down and sabotaged the entire industry.

Venezuela lost over 20 billion dollars in just little over two months. Then, after that happened, it was an illegal strike anyway, but they also sabotaged all the equipment. The industry had to be rescued manually. It was functioning originally in an automated way, but since everything had been sabotaged, codes had been switched, there had been control remotely that was basically running the system from the United States, and so everything had to be restructured entirely. All those that were involved, because they violated their contracts, were out of the industry forever basically.

So, yeah, it played an immense role in the beginning years of the Chávez administration in terms of all the destabilization that was going on. Now, of course, the industry is pretty firmly under the control, as it should be, of the state. But there are still pockets that exist within it a very extensive company that sabotage and it is Venezuela's lifeblood. Of course the most vulnerable part of the government is the oil industry. The fact that, even more so today, those funds are used for social programs in the country, so it's always a target.

That's why on May 24th the state department imposed sanctions against Venezuela's oil company PDVSA. The sanctions really have no teeth at all. They're just sending a message to the world that it's dangerous to do business with Venezuela, which is what the state department actually declared with the sanctions.

Sheehan: Except the US is still buying oil from Venezuela.

Golinger: That's correct!

Sheehan: So the US is in Venezuela? But the sanctions were put on because of some sanctions with Iran, I guess. I think, "how rude of Venezuela to put Venezuela's interests over the interests of the United States."

Golinger: (Laughing) Well, actually, that is precisely the mentality of those running the US government. In fact, beyond that, imposing internal US legislation on other countries, which is not even legitimate under international law, US law has no jurisdiction or bearing on another country.

Yet the US, because they have the capacity to impose pressure via economic means or political means, tends to use its legislation to influence other countries, and other countries often abide by what the US is requesting. In the case of Venezuela, Venezuela is a sovereign state and has declared itself so and remains so and will remain so. President Chávez is pretty adamant about the fact that Venezuela is no longer a colony of the US. Venezuela has the right not to have relations with any country in the world, just like the United States does. Those sanctions as far as Venezuela is concerned, have absolutely no legality whatsoever.

Sheehan: Well, absolutely. That brings up a couple of questions and I think that there are challenges to the continued viability of the Bolivarian Revolution and what's happening in Venezuela.

The first one is, many supporters of Chávez and the revolution, their question is, if something does happened to him, is the revolution strong enough to continue without the leadership that he's provided?

Golinger: Well, President Chávez of course is a very charismatic and powerful leader—there's no denying that whatsoever. Of course his leadership has been crucial in uniting different sectors and organizations of Venezuelan society to build this revolution. But, at the same time, the revolution was in motion before Hugo Chávez came to power.

The Revolution in Venezuela is really something that is being built and being maintained and advanced by the people of Venezuela. So while yes, his leadership is important, it would be very difficult to imagine Venezuela taking a step backward instead of continuing to advance forward. Of course if Chávez were no longer president at some point, which he won't be president forever, that's not the objective or a possibility. So someone else will be in power in Venezuela some day. Certainly things will change in terms of that particular aspect of the revolution and that level of leadership.

One of the main objectives of the Bolivarian Revolution in Venezuela has been transferring power to the people. That entire concept is based on the notion that the people of Venezuela are going to be those that are basically running their own country and that are implementing all of the different policies and initiatives. While, yes again, Chávez's leadership is very important, there's a whole new generation of Venezuelans that have been growing up in a different model over the past decade that have a different vision of their country, that have a stronger identity. Their identity has been recovered, has been dignified as being Venezuelan because of this particular revolution. So, therefore, I think that there is an entire generation of leaders that are growing up in Venezuela and that are going to be the ones running the show.

While everyone would love Chávez to be around, those that

support him, as long as he can be, I don't think it is a question of, "Well if he is no longer there, there is no revolution." Then that would mean there never has been a revolution. So I think that absolutely things will continue, they will change obviously in terms of the dynamic, but there's no question. This is a revolution of the people, and the people will continue to be the ones that are changing and transforming their country.

Sheehan: I just really want to thank you for your time and all the information that you always bring to the show. The last question would be: An economy based on oil is always very unstable. I mean it is good right now, but there's been many years where it hasn't been good, so that means that the economy fluctuates based on oil. What steps is Venezuela taking to transition itself off of an economy based on fossil fuel?

Golinger: The Venezuelan government has been trying to diversify industry now in the country and that's sort of the next phase of this transformation of the revolution. Building new industry, focusing on, Venezuela is not just oil wealthy, it has a wide variety of minerals and metals in the country that are now being produced, and the idea is not just to produce raw materials, but also to build factories in Venezuela so that Venezuela can produce products like automobiles and a whole slew of other industries and products. So there's a diversification in that sense of industry.

And then there's also a focus again on agriculture, which was abandoned in the early 20th century because of the focus on oil. So Venezuela is rebuilding its agricultural industry in order to reduce its dependence on imports, but also to become a power in terms of agricultural production.

So, to have a wide variety of exports, as well as to supply the people of Venezuela. At the same time, though, Venezuela has the largest reserves and though someday they will dry up, they will at least be around for another hundred years. When they are drying up throughout the Middle East, they will still be in Venezuela. Venezuela also has a large amount of water reserves, which of course many say is the next target of powerful interests around the world. So, yeah, there are a lot of initiatives going on to decrease the dependence on oil as the only product that Venezuela produces. Absolutely.

Sheehan: Well, and I think we as a people have to decrease our dependence on oil and oil-based products also. Just one last thing, I would like you to talk about the housing project in Venezuela. I think that is a very exciting thing that the government and the people are getting involved in right now.

Golinger: Absolutely, it is a wonderful initiative called Gran Mission Housing Venezuela. It is a government program that is involving millions of people as well as in terms of creating the program itself — training those as part of the mission.

Housing Venezuela is a mission work social program in terms of creating jobs, and the idea is to provide job training to people so they can take part and build cooperatives, to create cooperatives, to be involved in the construction of the more than 2 million homes that are being built in Venezuela presently and are expected to be completed in their totality within the next 6 years.

The idea, of course, is to address the housing crisis, the long-term housing crisis that exists in Venezuela. There's a big difference, for example, in the way the housing crisis has been handled in the United States and in the case of Venezuela. In the case of the United States the government bailed out banks, bailed out financial institutions, insurance companies, mortgage institutions, and let all the people who lost their homes, just left them on the streets—no help to them. But in the case of Venezuela it's been the exact opposite.

We've also had scandals with companies that have committed fraud, that have scammed people, real estate companies scamming people, Banks that have also committed fraud and have been mismanaging funds. Most of the banks involved in any kind of illicit activity were actually liquidated in Venezuela— were intervened by the state—were either liquidated or nationalized. Customer savings were all protected.

In the case of the housing industry, those companies involved in any kind of fraud have been mainly nationalized or somehow taken over or expropriated. The housing programs are all continuing in order to ensure that no one loses their home, or their future home, in the case of construction projects.

There's also been a problem last year—we had heavy rains, left over 130 thousand people homeless because of the flooding. So those have been the first priority in terms of providing homes. What the state is doing is ensuring homes are available, so many are being built because the housing doesn't exist. So apartments, homes all throughout the country, are being built by state, joint private and public enterprises, and then the homes will be distributed on a need basis—dealing first with those displaced by the rain.

It's not something that is just a gift. They're examining every person, every family individually. What's their income capacity? So do they have the capacity to put down a 5 percent deposit, a 10 percent deposit, a 30 percent deposit, no deposit? So no down payment is necessary if the person or family can't afford it, and then they are given a low-interest loan, a very low-interest loan, under 5 percent. It's to be able to pay off the cost of the housing. The housing, depending also on the income, if the person is basically below the poverty line or at the poverty line, then the government will subsidize 70 percent of the loan and will only be 30 percent which the person or family has to pay. So it's on an individual basis.

There are brigades going throughout the country going door-to-door visiting people that signed up for the program and are evaluating each case. It's also applying to those who currently have homes but need renovations that have problems with the internal structure. The government will provide a subsidy to be able to do that. The idea overall is that the government of Venezuela wants its people to be healthy and happy and stable. Every one knows having your own home is a huge part of feeling safe in your residence and your country. So Venezuela puts people before profits. This is another sign of that.

Sheehan: Eva thank you so much for being on Cindy Sheehan's Soapbox. We really appreciate your work and your time in coming on and sharing all of this information with us.

Golinger: Well thank you Cindy. Any time.

* * *

You Wanna Know What's What in the Middle East?

This is a transcript of an interview I did with journalist, Robert Fisk, on September 26, 2010. It isn't specifically about The

Bolivarian Revolution or Hugo Chávez, but I include it to show the similarity of US foreign policy in the Middle East, compared to Latin America.

Thanks to Robert Fisk; and Dede Miller for this transcript.

Sheehan: Robert Fisk, welcome to Cindy Sheehan's Soapbox. My first question is, what is the likelihood, or what do you think is the likelihood, that the US or Israel or the US *and* Israel will strike Iran's nuclear facilities soon?

Fisk: My crystal ball was broken quite a long time ago. It's a fact that quite soon after Obama became President he sent some pretty important Generals to Tel Aviv—that's where the Israeli Ministry of Defense is; it's not in Jerusalem—to tell them don't, don't, don't attack Iran; you're on your own if you want to do it. But of course they won't be on their own. If the Israelis attack Iran, the Iranians have said very specifically, and militarily it makes complete sense, from their point of view, that they would attack US forces in Afghanistan and Iraq and in the Gulf. And the reality is Americans are still fighting in Iraq. I mean they have 50,000 non-combat troops who have already been in combat 5 times. They can't take on a third war. They can hardly handle two. So it's not in America's interest to have a war with Iran, but it may be in Israel's interest and then we would bring in Americans again, and so on.

The real issue is, do we really, really think they will develop a nuclear missile or nuclear arms, and if they do, does it matter? I mean, you know, if you live in the Middle East, as I do, it's quite clear if you have a nuclear weapon you're not going to get invaded. We're not going to bomb North Korea, for example, or Pakistan, because they've got a bomb. So it's quite logical for any Muslim power, for example, if you want to prevent invasion or domination or attack by the west, get hold of a nuclear bomb. Just one.

And, anyway, it's not crackpots like Ahmadenijad the "president" of Iran who control nuclear weapons. It is much more serious people. And the idea that Iran is going to use them to destroy Israel and the whole of Palestine as well, and then get destroyed itself, is pretty ridiculous. But, you know, that danger is out there.

One of the things we do have to remember—it shouldn't be exaggerated, but it shouldn't be forgotten—is that we do have the most right-wing Israeli government in power at the moment. And people like Lieberman, the foreign minister, I put them in the same crackpot box as Ahmadinejad and Gaddafi.

So these are not, just as we have some odd characters in Tehran, we have some very odd characters in Jerusalem. Can we rely upon them for what we like to call common sense?—a very western expression. I don't know. Of course not only will Israel bring in the Americans if it attacked Iran, I think it would be very odd if the Hezbollah—forget Hamas and their tin-pot rockets—if Hezbollah did not respond in southern Lebanon, then of course, you're going to have a war involving Shiites and Americans. In Iraq it's the Sunnis; in Afghanistan it's the Sunnis. Now you're going to bring in the Shiites as well.

But, you know, all along one of the problems here is that there is this kind of —I mean, I come backwards and forwards to America all the time, sometimes 14 times a year—and somewhere over the Atlantic I fly through this sort of screen, and when I land in Washington or San Francisco or wherever, the Middle East is not the place I live in anymore. It's some fantasy world here that people don't talk about or have much knowledge of. The people who live there know of the history of course—we don't. So, decisions taken in Washington about Iran and decisions taken in Tehran about Washington are often very weirdly out of sync. The Iranians actually understand us much better than we understand them. But that won't stop an attack on Iran.

I rather think there would not be. But then again I have twice been wrong about the 14 wars I have covered in the Middle East. But the other 12 times I got it right. So I don't think there will be at the moment. That's my feeling, but as I said, my crystal ball is in little glass pieces all over the floor.

Sheehan: Robert, do you think there is more of a likelihood for a war between Israel and Hezbollah in the near future?

Fisk: I had the dubious pleasure of being present in the last Hezbollah Israeli war in 2006. It ended, of course, with George Bush claiming the Israelis had won, which is another fantasy.

The Israelis know they didn't win—they were humiliated, their armor was blown to pieces in Lebanon, their soldiers were shot down. They couldn't defend their own cities. The Hezbollah claimed it was a divine victory.

Well I was on the road to Southern Lebanon it didn't feel much like a divine victory or any other kind to me. But clearly the Israelis lost. I am not sure the Hezbollah won, but the Israelis lost.

When I talk to Hezbollah now, and I talk to Hezbollah fighters in the South, not just leadership people who are put in front of TV cameras, they clearly are looking forward to a second round to convince the world that they really did win last time. When I was in Israel a few weeks ago I went to the Herzliya Conference, which is where all the Israeli political right meet to make long speeches.

I flew into Israel to the Herzliya Conference to report on it and met a lot of people who pop up on my TV screen in Beirut raging about Lebanon. I came away with the distinct impression, especially after listening to the Deputy Chief of Staff of the IDF, the Israeli Army, ta king about Lebanon, of which he seemed to have very little political grasp. I came away with the distinct impression that the Israelis want to repair their shattered image from 2006 and have another go at Hezbollah.

One of the things we have to remember in all these affairs is the Israeli/Arab wars is that the Israeli Army has actually performed lamentably for decades now. They haven't won a war in 37 years. 1973 was the last real victory the Israelis won.

The invasion of Lebanon in 1978 petered out in a long bloody occupation. '82 was a disastrous massacre. The 1993 bombardment was hopeless. 1996 ended in the Qana Massacre. 2006 ended in another massacre with massive casualties. But I think the Israelis want another go and I think Hezbollah wants another go. I fear of course, as usual, there's two things that will happen if that does take place. The civilian casualties will be grossly disproportionate. Vast areas of Lebanon will be destroyed infrastructure, road, and of course will be rebuilt afterwards. And the State Department, and I absolutely promise you this, the State Department will call on both sides to exercise restraint and both sides will know that they are lying. And the Israelis will tell America to get off side until they end up in another massacre or tragedy and then they will be pleading for a UN ceasefire and then the old UN donkey will clip clop in over the corpses and rubble and we will have another ceasefire until the next war and that's how it goes on. If that seems cynical it's because I live there.

Sheehan: Well, since you do live in the region, what do you think the implications are for the recent massive arms sale to Saudi Arabia and the Emirates from the United States?

Fisk: Well it's laughable. We all know, who live in the region, the Saudis can't use all this equipment. I mean 60 billion dollars. Funny, I slipped it into my file. I don't use Google or the Internet. I have real paper and books. I slipped it into my arms file and out popped another clipping from 12 years ago saying America was going to sell 60 billion dollars worth of arms to Saudi Arabia.

I go to Saudi Arabia. You can see this stuff lying with sheets over it so sand doesn't get in the works. By and large the Saudis can't use all this equipment. It has to be used by the Americans or some other air forces brought in to practice on it. But it's a prestige thing and part of the relationship of the Saudis to the Americans, you protect us and we'll buy your weapons, we'll keep you solvent. Look, quite apart from the oil and that's how the system works. It's totally corrupt, it helps nobody. It does not help the Saudi population. It certainly doesn't help the Iranians who they think they are defending themselves against, or we have to persuade them they are. It helps the American arms manufacturers; it helps the economy of the weapons manufacturers. Not much else here. But that's the way the system works. You know, it is one of the awful clichés one of the famous clichés. The famous Eisenhower quote about the Military Industrial Complex is correct and remains correct. Although like Chomsky's Manufacturer's Consent, it's become so true that nobody remembers it anymore.

Sheehan: What do you think will be the outcome of the peace talks between the US, Israel, and Palestine?

Fisk: First of all, we were told these latest meetings of Clinton, Obama, Mahmoud Abbas, Netanyahu and, heaven spare us, Blair as well, 5 to 11, the last chance of peace, etc. If it was so important why wasn't it held two months ago or five months ago? Why now?

Why, well because of the mid-term elections. This is yet another ploy and as usual the Arabs and Israelis are trotted out to play their role in the theatre, then they will be put to one side and there will be another war and we will say how did it happen and so forth. No long term planning. Those days are gone.

If you go to the West Bank, as I say, I was in the West Bank, Israel and Gaza last week, it's perfectly obvious that there is no chance for a Palestinian State. There will be a one State solution and the State I think will be called Israel.

And those Palestinians, who remain in the borders of that state which will stretch from the Jordan River to the Mediterranean, they will either disappear and leave to Syria or Europe, or San Francisco or Washington. Or they will stay and be the guest workers for the Israelis.

You see, the key is what is known as Area C. Under the Oslo agreement Area C comprises about 62% of the West Bank a "putative Palestinian State." In this area, Israel has full occupational control. Other areas there's shared responsibilities. And in one or two particular cities like Ramallah the Palestinians in theory, unless the Israelis stage a raid, are in control.

But Area C now is effectively annexed off to Israel. When I went there, for example, quite apart from the fact that Jewish Colonies, which they are, forget the word settlements, continue to expand to thicken in size. I was actually traveling with Amir Hass, who of course is the very admirable and fine Israeli journalist from Haaretz.

All of the villages we went to the Palestinian Muktas met us and there were lots of cups of tea, and then they produced this huge file of documents from the Israeli occupational authorities in Hebrew. Signed, although the signatures were illegible, saying that this man cannot build another story on his house or else his house will be destroyed. This man cannot build another story. So the families can't expand, they can't get married, they of course they will go to Jordan, Lebanon, somewhere else.

One of the weirdest laws is that the Palestinians in these villages near the sea, 62% cannot dig more than 3 inches into the ground. This is an obvious problem because then they cannot operate sewage or wate,r but they cannot put up electricity poles because you can't put a pole 3 inches into the ground, it will fall over. So what they've done, they've got these huge concrete blocks and laid them on the earth and stuck the electricity poles into the concrete block. Now, how long do you keep hanging on in the face of what is clearly not only harassment, it's oppression?

When you talk to the Israelis at the check point they say, "Yes, yes, they can not dig more than 3 inches in case they put a bomb in the ground." So clearly Area C, 62% of the West Bank, cannot be inside a Palestinian State.

This means that as opposed to what we believe which is that Mahmoud Abbas is generously being allowed to negotiate for 22% of mandate Palestine, the original Palestine when the Brits were there. He's actually negotiating for about 10.8 or 10.9 percent of Mandate Palestine. And that ain't no state. It is not viable. It is not workable, its not secure, it can't work.

So I think, you know, the problem is that public opinion, partly because of us journalists and our endless waffling of this peace process, it never was a peace process to begin with; they still believe there is hope. That there is light at the end of the tunnel, usual clichés, its gone, Palestine is gone and there isn't going to be, I don't believe there will be a Palestinian State.

I think there will one state and it will be called Israel and the project will thus be completed. Now whether in the long term you can hold on to them.

I meet Jewish Americans, particularly in California and different parts of America who all but say, they say quite frankly, you know this Middle Eastern thing is a project, Zionist, Israeli, call it what you want, which may or may not work. For them security is here. I think if I was a Jewish American I would stay in America, and I only say that because many Jewish Americans tell me that is their choice too. But the idea that Israel is going to, even if it does effectively take all the Arab land, which militarily it has already anyway, the idea that it is going to survive indefinitely, well, we don't know.

Everything at the end of the day depends on the relationship with the United States, and as long as America gives it unconditional, uncritical support to Israel, right or wrong, there will be no peace. And that of course is a danger not just for the Arabs, but the Israelis as well.

There are many Israelis of course who believe this constant colonial expansion is going to destroy their home. I think they are right in saying that, but they are not necessarily a majority. One of the problems you have as a journalist who goes in and out of Israel, I mean I go to Israel from Lebanon via Jordan or Cypress, is that when I arrive you go to Tel Aviv, which is a very European City, lovely restaurants, good music, I go to the art gallery, I mean I appreciate lots of the things about Israeli culture and society. And of course I go and seek out all those nice lefties and liberal Israelis who say the kind of things I want to be said about Israel. But when I get on the bus up to Jerusalem I don't hear the same voices. There are settlers; there are Israelis who are not actually particularly educated. They may be immigrants from Russia; they haven't learned Hebrew very well. Their views of Arabs are pretty much what you hear form Hamas about the Israelis.

So it comes down to the old question countless books are written about, what is this country Israel? Who lives in it? Who are these people? And Israelis ask these questions all the time in their newspapers. They are preoccupied by it and rightly so actually. But when you have a country and this crazy political system, I mean, poor old Israelis to have disproportional representation constantly producing these crazed minority governments. In this country, with all these nuclear weapons. It's a pretty sorry situation. I don't know, I get up every morning in Beirut and I hear the palm trees swaying and the Mediterranean sloshing until the cars come and start hooting. I wait and wonder where is the explosion today I ask myself.

The most dangerous thing at the moment, THE most dangerous thing is that our masters, our leaders, the Obamas, the Bushes, the Blairs, the Camerons. They're still promoting this total fantasy that there can still be peace in the Middle East. And there isn't going to be. If we continue on this path there will continue to be continual war. As we have seen since WWII in the Middle East the wars have gotten steadily bigger, wider, worse entangling more and more countries. Now involving directly of course since 9/11 the United States, actually since before 9/11. The days where we can go on colonial adventures and sit happily at home are gone. But we don't realize that.

Sheehan: You've called President Ahmadinejad of Iran a "crack pot," what do you think about Hamas?

Fisk: I have a very cynical view of Hamas because they are a very cynical organization and very arrogant.

You see, first of all, let's run the narrative of history through from the beginning.

In 2006 the Palestinians were urged to have a democratic election. George Bush said "wonderful, have a democracy." So the Palestinian went to vote, pesky Palestinians voted for the wrong people, they voted for Hamas. They didn't vote for Hamas because they wanted an Islamic Republic. They voted for Hamas because they were sick and tired of the corruption of Mahmoud Abbas and Arafat and the whole Palestinian old fogies from Fatah.

It was brought home to me once, I was in Jerusalem and I got a call from Fatah "one of our officials' home has been shelled by an Israeli tank," I rushed down from my home in Jerusalem. There was the home, there was the hole, and there was the Israeli tank. But what struck me when I went into the house amid the rubble was all these gold plated taps in the bathroom.

There was the story. You don't vote for people like that, you vote for people who are clean.

Anyway then, 2007 Hamas takes over very bloodily in the Gaza Strip. And then they will not conform to the Oslo agreement. Their argument of course, which was quite logical, was well, the Israelis haven't conformed. They had been renegotiating Oslo and all these other places for a long time. But of course Hamas are not going to start out by acknowledging everything that Arafat did and then becoming the PLO or the Palestinian authority. But they've got very big heads.

You know, it is a very corrupt organization, Hamas. They think they are the Hezbollah of the south. They're not, they are nothing like Hezbollah. I remember one day there was this very big funeral in Gaza and all the Palestinians were shooting in the air. I remember watching this with a Hezbollah fighter in Lebanon and I said, "Hussein, what do you think of this?" He said, "Well, we sympathize with them because they are martyrs, but why do they waste all of this ammunition?" It was a very interesting example of when you have a professional guerilla army as opposed to this ragtag bunch in Gaza.

Then you see you will remember certain other things. Why are they really firing all these stupid tin-pot missiles into Israel to provoke an assault? Okay, you can provoke an assault if you can then fight the Israelis, but they couldn't fight the Israelis. You know they killed at least 35 alleged Palestinian collaborators but only killed 13 Israelis of whom two were Arab Israelis, by the way. And then they lost 1,300 of there own people, most of them civilians. That is not a great victory. I mean, Hezbollah were very, very cynical and rightly so about Hamas performance. They were arrogant. They thought they could beat the Israelis and they ran away. The Israelis did not find their soldier so he was hid very well.

But Hamas, I've been down these tunnels, by the way, one of them has got a railway line—the tunnels that go to Egypt. And Egypt, of course, is playing the colonial role of doing what the masters want as well by sealing off Gaza.

But these tunnels, Hamas takes a cut on the profits of at least five million a year. Some people put that at quadruple at 500 million a year and they need that money. The word I hear in Gaza, everybody profits. The Egyptians profit, they are backhanders to the Israelis to make sure they don't actually bomb all the tunnels cause you've got to keep some of them open. So the tunnel system is a massive financial scam and Hamas holds the tap on it.

The reason I think Hamas turns back food when it does come in from Israel is because it is losing its scams on the tunnels. They're losing taxation you see. So it's okay, you can bring a few weapons through, you can bring donkeys and paint them like tigers at the zoo. Whatever you want to do. But at the end of the day Hamas is a totally compromised corrupt organization. It's not the massive terrorist organization that Israel makes it out to be.

I mean Israel—I was in Gaza when Arafat was still pouncing around Beirut pretending to be the center of Arab Nationalism. And I was actually present when the Israeli Gaza commander—because they had a military base in Gaza, a big one—was negotiating with Hamas in a mosque, in which I was present, and encouraging Hamas to build more mosques in Gaza as a counter balance to the horrible super terrorist, Arafat, who was up in Beirut. Then of course as we know the super terrorist turned out to be a super statesman and went to the White

House on the night Hamas mosques were filled with super terrorists who had been talking to the Israelis.

In 1992-93 Israel expelled hundreds of Palestinians into Lebanon and they were stuck on the border. The Lebanese would not let them in.

There's a very funny incident there, I used to go down and talk to some every few weeks, see how they were doing, they were cold, living in tents. One day I went there and I mentioned to them that I was going to Israel the next day via Cypress on this occasion. One of them got up; a big bearded man and rushed off to a tent. When he came back he said " Mr. Robert would you like Mr. Perez's telephone number?" So I said yes, and took it down and it was his home telephone number. So here you go here are the elite of Israeli political society obviously talking to these Hamas men who were being abused on Israeli radio as the worst kind of terrorists in the history of the world. Of course one of the things you must realize is that all these people talk to each other. Hamas talks to the Israelis, the Israelis talk to Hamas. The Israelis talk to the Syrian Secret Service directly, not just through Turkey and so on. But of course the newspaper version is that little Israel is fighting this vast sea of terrorism and so on. It's not like that. But this is a good story. It's easy. It's not controversial and journalists, they can get away with it so they did.

Sheehan: You've lived the Middle East for at least 30 years. What keeps you going in that part of the world?

Fisk: I suppose observing the folly of mankind is not a – it's a difficult thing to shake off. It's not like an addiction but one does, you know, I can turn on Al Jazeera or even occasionally the BBC and hear the latest statements from Bush or Obama or

Blair, they are so outrageous it is almost like a comedy theatre to listen to. A smile does cross my face.

But if you really want to know why I really do it. I was 29 when I went to the Middle East. I am 64 now and I am still doing the same job, living in the same house, almost the same salary. I suppose the answer is really a bit like reading a great historical novel. You know, you are reading *War and Peace, Battle of Borodino,* what would happen to Pierre? You're reading late in bed and it is almost midnight, and I'll just finish this chapter. Then you find yourself reading the next chapter. Then you say you will just finish the next chapter. Before you know you look up and see the sun coming through the curtains. It's dawn and you've read all through the night. Because you want to see what happens next you see. I think that is why I still work as a journalist in the Middle East. I want to know what happens next. It won't be nice, but I am just desperate to see what happens in this path of human folly.

Sheehan: We're making a documentary about Venezuela and the demonization of President Chávez and his Bolivarian revolution. You've seen demonization of Arab countries and Arab leaders and it correlates to what's happening in South America. What do you think the US should be doing in the Middle East?

Fisk: Look, one of the themes of modern Middle Eastern History is that if you want to be a surviving dictator you've got to work for us— Mubarak, King Hussein, Little King Abdullah, the King of Morocco, the President of Algeria, Gaddafi, now.

If you invade the right countries, like Iran 1980, we will support a dictator. We don't call him a dictator we call him a pro-western strongman on the AP wire. If you invade the wrong country like Kuwait then we will biff them. When King Idriss was overthrown by Gaddafi, the British foreign office wholeheartedly supported this fine young army Colonel called Moammar Gaddafi. He loved him.

The he got involved in the IRA, then he was involved in the bombing of Berlin night clubs, so we biffed him too and had to bomb him. Then he said he was giving up nuclear weapons even though the average Libyan doesn't seem to know how to repair a lavatory in a Tripoli Hotel, and we love him again, just because he is as much a crackpot as Ahmadinejad and Lieberman of Israel and all the rest.

So we switch on the bestiality system when these people go into bay. And usually the reason they go into bay, Nasser for instance at the time of nationalization of the Suez, Saddam in Kuwait, and so on, is when they've donned the clothes of nationalism, have said that they now speak for the Arab people or the Venezuelan people in the case of Chávez. Then that gets very dangerous because we are the people in the west decide who runs these countries and how they behave.

Egypt is a good example because it has always been obedient. Sadat crossed the canal but he actually did it rather well and afterwards he wanted peace, so that was okay, with Israel.

But the demonization is easy to switch on and off and usually you use WWII. Saddam became the Hitler of the Tigress and we even called Nasser the Mussolini of the Nile in 1956 during the Suez war. I know the same comments have been made about Chávez as well.

And always when semi-dictators or slightly odd people—and Chávez is a bit odd, we have to admit this—decide that they will do what the people want, rather than what the west wants, then we will surround them and threaten them and that builds up their stature even more and that projects them on to a world stage that makes them friends with Ahmadinejad and Gaddafi and a host of the worlds crackpot summit forum: Which alas, sometimes I have to cover as a journalist.

But I mean, there is no doubt that American Foreign policy is straightforward. You have your set of dictators and if they step out of line, you bat them over the head and hope that they don't, and if they don't ,you depose them and they'll end up hanged like Saddam. But I think that basically what American policy is if you strip it down and look at it from the other point of view. But again, you see we are not talking about the most important issue, which is of course oil and control of oil. Control of oil doesn't mean owning it or even owning the rights to explore reserves. It means insuring for the foreseeable future, i.e., eternity that the flow of oil continues at current or future necessary rates. And that of course is what Iraq was about. People can say it was about democracy, weapons of mass destruction and getting rid of Saddam. At the end of the day no matter how awful Saddam was, if the main national export product of Iraq was asparagus or potatoes the 82nd Airborne would not have gone to Baghdad and that is a fact.

Sheehan: What about Afghanistan? Why is the US and NATO in Afghanistan?

Fisk: Because major super powers want to be destroyed in Afghanistan. They always go there and they always get destroyed. The British did it in 1842; they did it again in 1878. We almost did it in 1919. The Russians did it in 1979, got thrown out in '88 and then we come up in 2001.

Poor old Afghans I keep saying, poor old Afghans. Why are we in Afghanistan? It is preposterous human folly. Well, you know you can look and say gas pipelines from the former Soviet Muslim Republics to Pakistan, etc. I think there is a bit more to this; you see, it's not just about some immediate post 9/11 anger over Al Qaeda.

It was a very odd way in which Taliban had to be destroyed because they wouldn't give us Bin Laden. Although for a period they might have avoided destruction. I mean we would have turned our backs on Burkas and women's rights and gender equality and all these other projects, which we have. And indeed we know at one point the Taliban were being courted in Houston of all places because we wanted them to be involved in this wonderful gas project that would bring so much happiness and prosperity to Afghanistan.

I think, in the end, we went there because you are an Empire and we were an Empire and the Lion still has a few whiskers. The same applies very much in Iraq, as well as the oil and the fantasy in Israel. Empires have to project power. If they are bitten by a mosquito, they must kill the mosquito and smash their fist so hard there are no more mosquitoes afterwards.

The projection of power is the lifeblood of Empires. The Romans did it. The Romans did it more wisely because they regarded everyone outside their borders as Barbarians, which is what we do, Taliban, Hamas, Islamic Jihad, Al Qaeda. But once they grabbed the country, they made all the people citizens of Rome.

I once tried to explain to a CIA officer in Kufa in Iraq that if the Americans had come to Iraq and offered all the Iraqis US passports there'd been no insurgency. The Iraqi's would not have flooded into JFK. They would have said, "My goodness, the Americans really do love us." That would be the end. But of course that wasn't going to be a policy that commended itself to the Bush administration or indeed to Mr. Blair. Because we don't love them, we don't even care about them. The Romans at least went through the motions. I'm not recommending crucifixion here but, Empires work this way.

I remember once, this is going to Iraq; South of Baghdad I was investigating the murders of some Red Cross drivers. I was talking to an Iraqi family who I think saw the murder on the horrible, throat-cutting Highway 8. The ground had started to tremble and up the road there was one of these big Brigade turn overs, largest since WWII. Up the road came this unstoppable, never ending, hour after hour convoy of M1-A1 Abrams Tanks, Bradley fighting armored vehicles, truck after truck, all with soldiers with their rifles pointed out like porcupine quills, shades over their eyes, and all these Apache helicopters over top.

I remember I sat on the side of the road with this poor Iraqi family that is just dumbstruck at this, and thinking, "Two thousand years ago if I had been a reporter, I would have been a little more to the west in Lebanon and it would have been the tramp of Roman legions I would have heard coming past me endlessly on the road."

We can go to Baghdad. We will go to Baghdad, and we will send our armies through the lands of Sumeria where civilization began you see. Empires are real. They breathe. They are very dangerous things too, like governments. I think that in a way Afghanistan beckons in this poisonous way to Empires to go and show that they breathe you see.

We have surges now. Surges just means reinforcements because we're losing but we build it up into this massive Tsunami like unstoppable force. Like spikes and valleys where it comes down and goes up again, we mean increases in violence and their not going down. That's the whole problem. But there you go; I think it's about oil in Iraq. I think it's about Empire in Iraq and Afghanistan. Who knows in Iran and Venezuela?

I don't know how you switch it off. Historically, there have been foreign invaders or economic collapse. I did Roman history and classics for my first degree, along with Linguistics. I still read about the fall of the Roman Empire. Not the movie or Hollywood version. It is true that the Goths, the Ostrogoths and the Visigoths did a lot of invading of Roman territory, but it was the Roman economy that brought it down. It collapsed in basically valueless products. And then you know the postal system didn't work so well and the bread didn't arrive from Lebanon. So that's also worth bearing in mind.

It was, after all, the final death of the British Empire was basically the end of the second World War when Britain went bankrupt and the Americans said, "Okay it's the end of lend lease, we'd like the money now please." The idea that Empires collapse because of bearded men that get into the country on Visas issued by the CIA, or because their soldiers get beat in Afghanistan, which like Vietnam does have a very critical point. At the moment the situation is that America and Britain are not losing sufficient numbers to have the kind of serious effect it might otherwise have in the country. I mean it's nothing like Vietnam casualties.

I'm very struck by when I am in America, for example, that I see in the paper everyday, you know the *New York Times*, *Chronicle*, the *LA Times*, the little list of dead, Spc. so and So, age 24–26, and its almost like people killed in a storm or the flash flood last night. It is like it is a natural disaster now cause it's not big enough to make an impact.

Sheehan: Tell my listeners the story you told me earlier about Chávez and the leader of Hezbollah, Nasrallah.

Fisk: What was particularly funny at the time, when the Israeli bombardment ended at Southern Lebanon with actually flooding the country with cluster bombs, we went into the villages, some of which were refuse, heaps of rubble and they stank as the bodies of villagers were dead under the rubble. But where the Mukta had survived, and there were a few winded Hezbollah lying around in the streets, too. But where the Mukta, the village leaders had survived, Fisk would always rush up and say, "So what do you think the situation is here?" And they would proclaim their everlasting love of Hezbollah. And I'd say, do you like Nasrallah the leader of Hezbollah? They would always say, "We like two people. We like Nasrallah and we like Chávez." I was actually with a Washington Post reporter who doubled up with laughter each time. They all said this, they hadn't been prompted, they actually believed this. I said, "why" to one of them, I can't remember the name of the place, Rehan? Rihanna? I said to this guy, "Why do you like Chávez?" He said, "Because he is like Nasrallah, he really makes Bush angry."

Sheehan: While we were in Venezuela we interviewed one of the Deputy Foreign Ministers, Temir Porres, and I asked him if he thought that the US Empire would collapse probably sooner than later? His answer was, "I hope so!" What are your thoughts on that?

Fisk: One of the things we don't think enough about is America could, if it wanted to be, a great source of strength and goodness in the Middle East if it would get rid of it's obsessions of a democracy, about Israel and actually treat everyone with the same fairness, including Israel.

You've got to remember at the end of the first World War, which was partly fought to destroy the Ottoman Empire, you still had a vast stretch of land from the Mesopotamian Persian border, Iraq and Iran today, all the way to the Atlantic. And many US service officers in the State Department who were counsels to the dying Ottoman Empire, places like Beirut, Tripoli, Constantinople, they were all petitioning the State Department, as were the American NGO's (they were missionaries then), to have one modern Arab Nation that would become a democracy like the democracies of Europe and which the west would put all it's treasure and financial and medical help—not military —but all its economic power to bring in to be one Arab Nation united as a democracy.

Wilson died; isolationism set in on Congress and the House. And of course the British and the French had already chopped up the Middle East for themselves under the Sykes-Pekoe agreement and produced this wondrous, glorious success story that exists today. There was a moment when, and amazingly Arabs far apart from the Israelis still had this buried hope in America. That's why Obama got away with his initial months of saying, we're reaching out to Muslim world. Some of them actually believed it. All over again. After all the evidence, they believed it.

I went to see Obama in Cairo when he spoke, and it's funny, if you see these guys, as opposed to just watching it on a flat screen TV, you pay more attention to their words and there were lots of tripwires in his speech. The "relocation" of the

Palestinians in '48, like they got up in the morning and said, "Let's go to Lebanon." Its heart was in the right place and of course the Arab elites wanted this to work. It was very interesting. When he spoke at Cairo University I got into. The Egyptians present were all members of the sort of pro-regime, pro-American upper middle class elite of society. There was nobody there who was going to be shouting Islamic statements to Mr. Obama. Of course, it wasn't going to happen.

Made in the USA
Charleston, SC
09 June 2012